Understanding Financial

Stewardship

BY

Charles F. Stanley

Thomas Nelson

Since 1798

Published in Nashville, Tennessee, by Thomas Nelson, Inc., Publishers, and distributed in Canada by Word Communications, Ltd., Richmond, British Columbia.

Editing, layout, and design by Gregory C. Benoit Publishing, Old Mystic, CT

The Bible version used in this publication is THE NEW KING JAMES VERSION. Copyright 1979, 1980, 1982, Thomas Nelson, Inc., Publishers.

ISBN 1-4185-3335-1

Printed in the United States of America

HB 11.09.2017

Contents

A Fresh Look at Financial Stewardship

Many people think of the Bible as a book of inspiration and spiritual truths—and it certainly is that. But the Bible is also one of the most practical, down-to-earth books that has ever been written. It relates to every area of our lives, including the acquisition and use of money and material possessions. The Bible has a great deal to say about wealth and poverty, and what makes a person rich or poor. It contains eternal truths about the importance of giving, the necessity of receiving, and the way to prosperity.

As you study God's principles for good financial stewardship, I encourage you to go again and again to your Bible to underline phrases, highlight words or verses, and make notes in the margins to record the specific ways that God speaks to you. I believe in a well-marked Bible. My Bible is filled with dates, notes, and insights.

God's truth is for all people at all times, but the application of that truth to your life is always very personal and direct. Take note of the specific ways in which God admonishes, encourages, or directs you.

This book can be used by you alone or by several people in a small-group study. At various times, you will be asked to relate to the material in one of these four ways:

1. *What new insights have you gained?* Make notes about the insights that you have. You may want to record them in your Bible or in a separate journal. As you reflect back over your insights, you are likely to see how God has moved in your life.

2. *Have you ever had a similar experience?* Each of us approaches the Bible from a unique background—our own particular set of relationships and experiences. Our experiences do not make the Bible true—the Word of God is truth regardless of our opinion about it. It is important, however, to share our experiences in order to see how God's truth can be applied to human lives.

3. *How do you feel about the material presented?* Emotional responses do not give validity to the Scriptures, nor should we trust our emotions as a gauge for our faith. In small-group Bible study, however, it is good for participants to express their emotions. The Holy Spirit often communicates with us through this unspoken language.

4. *In what way do you feel challenged to respond or to act?* God's Word may cause you to feel inspired or challenged to change something in your life. Take the challenge seriously and find ways of acting upon it. If God reveals to you a particular need that He wants *you* to address, take that as "marching orders" from God. God is expecting you to *do* something with the challenge that He has just given you.

Start and conclude your Bible study sessions in prayer. Ask God to give you spiritual eyes to see and spiritual ears to hear. As you conclude your study, ask the Lord to seal what you have learned so that you will never forget it. Ask Him to help you grow into the fullness of the stature of Christ Jesus.

Again, I caution you to keep the Bible at the center of your study. A genuine Bible study stays focused on God's Word and promotes a growing faith and a closer walk with the Holy Spirit in *each* person who participates.

LESSON 1

What Is Your Net Worth?

꙰ In This Lesson ꙰

LEARNING: WHAT IS MY NET WORTH?

GROWING: WHAT DOES THE BIBLE SAY ABOUT PROSPERITY?

Net worth is a concept that most people understand solely in terms of finance—it refers to the numerical figure remaining after your debts have been subtracted from your assets. Ideally, the amount is a positive number, not a negative one. The larger the number, the richer you are thought to be from a human perspective.

Net worth from God's perspective is different. God sees the whole of your life when He views your prosperity. He doesn't divide your life into segments and evaluate you according to some kind of average of strengths and weaknesses. More important, God doesn't look at any numbers or other statistics when He calculates your worth. He looks instead at His immeasurable love for you and the sacrifice that Jesus Christ made on the cross. In that light, you are beyond any measurement that might be associated with value. (See John 3:16.)

Fully Vested for Prosperity

Once you have accepted Jesus Christ as your Savior and have received God's forgiveness for your sin, you are fully vested in God's total prosperity plan. You qualify fully for His promises related to prosperity and blessing. That isn't the case for nonbelievers. People who have not accepted Jesus Christ simply cannot experience full prosperity—according to God's definition of prosperity—primarily because being prosperous includes prosperity in the spiritual life.

You must understand these key concepts at the outset of this study:

1. Prosperity relates to your entire life. A person can be rich and still not be prosperous. When you think of blessing and prosperity, you must think in terms of life's whole—a harmony that has spiritual, mental, emotional, physical, financial, and relational dimensions.

2. Prosperity is God's plan for every believer. God's greatest desire is that you be a whole person. He desires to bless you and cause you to grow in every area of your life in a balanced and fruitful way. He wants you to fulfill His destiny on earth—and to do so as a whole person. God wants you to prosper. It is with this frame of mind that you should approach the subject of financial stewardship.

Financial Stewardship

Financial stewardship has to do with the way in which you use your resources to provide for your needs and for the needs of God's kingdom. Stewardship involves far more than your money, because your resources involve far more than money and material goods. Among your resources are your talents, experiences, creative ideas, energy, time, spiritual gifts, and much more. Your resources encompass the total you. God desires to bless all of you and to be directly involved in every area of your life, and He wants all of you to be actively involved in His plan for this world.

God has given you all that you have and all of your potential. All that you are and all that you will ever be are His gifts to you. His desire is that you will give back to Him all that you are and all that you hope to be. I have labeled this study *financial stewardship* for two reasons:

First, we are focusing on **material and financial resources.** That certainly doesn't mean that stewardship is limited to finances, but a complete study of stewardship would require far more than this book can contain.

Second, this study is concerned with **stewardship,** not merely finances. Stewardship involves all of the giving and receiving principles that apply to your relationship with God and your support of God's plan for your life and the lives of others. Stewardship implies a caretaker role. A good steward manages the resources of the master with the utmost care and concern.

Every person is a steward of God's gifts, including money and material goods. Therefore, financial stewardship is something with which all people are involved, whether they know it or not. You are a financial steward for your Master and Lord, Jesus Christ. God has a perfect plan for what you are to do with your money and material wealth. He has a plan for blessing you with an increase in money and material possessions, and for you to increase your ability to bless others. The goal in this study is to help you discover that plan of God.

No Separation

Many people have a mind-set that "business is business" and "church is church." They separate the two almost completely in their minds and sometimes in the way they act. They have differing attitudes toward money and toward worship. It may come as quite a jolt to your thinking

5

to face the reality of God's Word: God doesn't separate your business life from your spiritual life. The two are intricately connected.

Again, we go back to our understanding of prosperity. You simply cannot be prosperous if you are growing and bearing fruit in only one area of your life. Prosperity has to do with all your life. In a very practical way, God is just as concerned about your finances and your ability to meet your material needs as He is with your spiritual growth and development.

Many people have been taught incorrectly to think of money as being filthy lucre. They view finance and business as unspiritual matters, and certainly not anything that could ever be considered holy. They regard money and financial principles as subjects that should be outside the domain of the church.

Let me assure you, God doesn't see money as filthy. Money itself is neutral in His eyes. It is what we do with our money that counts before God. His desire is that our financial life become sanctified, which means that we deal with our finances in purity, governed by right motives, and in ways that are wholly acceptable to God. Furthermore, if church leaders had taught people through the years more about good financial stewardship based on principles in God's Word, many people would have been spared heartache and sorrow.

As a pastor, I have talked to thousands of people over the years who have shared with me their problems and difficulties. A very large percentage of the problems have been rooted in financial difficulty. Many people readily admit that their marital difficulties involve money. Others are heartbroken that they aren't prepared for retirement, unexpected illness, or major financial expenditures because they have never learned to manage their money according to God's principles. Still others are frustrated at being unable to do the ministry work that God has called them to do because they don't have the resources to meet their needs or the needs of their ministries—again, because they aren't living according to God's principles of sound financial stewardship.

Financial difficulties affect all areas of a person's life. You cannot have a major problem involving money without experiencing some degree of doubt or frustration in your mind, emotions, and relationships, including your relationship with God. It is good to talk about money and to discover what God has to say about its acquisition and use. It is good for you, and it is good for the church as a whole, to know God's will for the material life.

For Your Blessing

I've also discovered through the years that the minute a preacher begins to talk about money, many people jump to a conclusion that he wants their money. Furthermore, they suspect that the preacher wants their money for his use. Let me assure you at the very outset of this study that I don't want anything *from* you. At no time in this study will I ask you for a contribution or financial gift. Instead, I want something *for* you.

I want to see you blessed fully by God. I want to see you become a whole person and be prosperous in every area of your life. I want to see you fulfill your purpose on earth. I want to help you understand God's principles for good financial stewardship so you can begin to use them for your benefit.

God's principles for financial stewardship and prosperity are universal, eternal, and absolute. The specific ways in which God directs you to use your resources and to give of yourself are going to be personal, detailed, and specific. Trust God to be true to His Word. Trust Him to bless you. Trust Him to guide your stewardship of the gifts that He gives you. Let God be the Provider for your entire life, including your finances, and the Source of your prosperity.

🙠 What do you hope to learn about finances and stewardship? Are there money-related needs in your life for which you need God's answer?

🙠 In what areas have you struggled with money or stewardship in the past?

🙠 Today and Tomorrow 🙢

TODAY: MY "NET WORTH" IS DEFINED BY THE FACT THAT JESUS SHED HIS BLOOD FOR ME.

TOMORROW: I WILL SPEND TIME THIS WEEK REFLECTING ON HOW VALUABLE I AM IN GOD'S EYES.

Lesson 2

The Place of Money in Your Life

❧ In This Lesson ❧

LEARNING: IS IT MORE GODLY TO BE POOR THAN TO BE RICH?

GROWING: WHAT IS THE PROPER PLACE FOR MONEY IN A CHRISTIAN'S LIFE?

How much money can a Christian make and still be a Christian? How much money can a Christian have and still be spiritually minded? Is there an income level at which someone stops being obedient to God?

Such questions often enter into conversations about money and material wealth. Many people believe that money and spirituality are incompatible. Some of this belief comes from teachings related to two verses in the Bible.

A Blessing on Poverty?

The first verse is a very familiar one, from the passage of Scripture that we call the Beatitudes:

> Blessed are the poor in spirit,
> For theirs is the kingdom of heaven.

> —Matthew 5:3

People assume that, because this passage uses the word *poor*, the Lord was talking about people who were living in financial poverty. They conclude that poverty is linked to spirituality. These people have come to believe that being poor enables God can speak more clearly to them. Some even conclude that all poor people make it to heaven and that no rich people do.

We know from a very logical standpoint that this is not the case. Poor people don't stop being concerned about financial provision or cease desiring prosperity. If anything, they have a greater concern about meeting their material needs. Millions of people around the world awaken every morning with poverty foremost on their minds, and they spend long hours trying to eke out the barest of livings in their effort to stave off death, disease, and other horrible ravages of poverty. Poverty doesn't automatically make people more conscious of God or more spiritually minded. Furthermore, God doesn't stop speaking to the rich. He speaks to any person who has a listening heart, regardless of the balance in the checkbook.

Perhaps the more important issue, however, is that this verse doesn't say what people have come to think it says. Jesus refers to the "poor in spirit," not the poor in finances. He is speaking about those who are humble, who openly acknowledge their need of God's forgiveness. People must be poor in spirit—recognize that they need God and are spiritually destitute without Him—before they will ever turn to God and receive His forgiveness and love.

A lack of God's presence in our lives draws us to want a relationship with God, and when we come to that point, we are in the best position to accept Jesus Christ as our Savior and to receive God's forgiveness in our lives. When we accept Jesus, we enter into eternal life and a permanent home in heaven. Ours is the kingdom of heaven, as Jesus taught. A rich person can be humble before God, and a rich person can experience salvation and place all his trust in God. A poor person can be too angry with God to seek His forgiveness, and a poor person can reject God's offer of forgiveness and remain a sinner.

"But," some say, "there is a spirit of poverty, and those who have this spirit are more likely to turn to God." Yes, there is a spirit of poverty. It is a spirit that causes depression, dejection, and despair. It manifests itself in a lack of hope, and it can result in such fear and anxiety that faith is crushed. A spirit of poverty exists, but it is not a spirit that automatically causes a person to turn to God. Having a spirit of poverty is not at all the same as being "poor in spirit."

I've met people who grew up poor but never seemed to think of themselves as poor. They were surrounded by people who loved them and encouraged them in their faith. They look back on their financially meager childhoods and think of themselves as very rich in all the right things. I've also met people who grew up in wealthy homes, but who are impoverished when it comes to love and hope. They were given lots of material stuff, but not much love or attention. No, financial blessing doesn't automatically relate to the salvation of one's soul or a decision to follow in the footsteps of Jesus Christ. There is no inherent righteousness in poverty.

> Blessed are the poor in spirit, For theirs is the kingdom of heaven.
>
> —Matthew 5:3

❧ What does it mean to be "poor in spirit"? How is this different from being poor financially?

~ What does it mean that "theirs is the kingdom of heaven"? Why is this reserved for people who are "poor in spirit"?

The Poor with Us

A second verse that is often used to support the idea that poverty is linked to spirituality is this: "The poor you have with you always" (John 12:8). People have used this verse to conclude that God condones poverty. That is not what this verse says. There is no blessing attached with poverty, in this verse or any other verse. Jesus was pointing out to His disciples the reality of mankind as a whole, not God's desire for mankind. He was stating what is, not what God wishes.

Furthermore, we need to take this statement in the broader context of what was happening in the lives of Jesus and His disciples at that point. Jesus was in the house of Lazarus, whom Jesus had recently raised from the dead. Jesus was having supper with Lazarus and his sisters only a week before His crucifixion, and He knew that His time on earth was short. The Bible tells us:

> Mary took a pound of very costly oil of spikenard, anointed the feet of Jesus, and wiped His feet with her hair. And the house was filled with the fragrance of the oil. But one of His disciples, Judas Iscariot, Simon's son, who would betray Him, said, "Why was this fragrant oil not sold for three hundred denarii and given to the poor?" This he said, not that he cared for the

poor, but because he was a thief, and had the money box; and he used to take what was put in it. But Jesus said, "Let her alone; she has kept this for the day of My burial. For the poor you have with you always, but Me you do not have always."

—John 12:3–8

Jesus' main point was not that the poor are always in our midst, but that Judas's priorities were sorely misplaced. Judas claimed to be thinking of what could be given to the poor, when he was really concerned about having more money to embezzle. Judas had no sensitivity toward what God was about to do in Jesus' life; he had no sensitivity toward the motive of Mary's heart. Jesus clearly and accurately read Judas's intentions and stated just as clearly that any gift given out of sacrificial love is a worthy gift. Jesus is not bestowing any honor upon poverty.

Why did Mary anoint the Lord's feet? Why did she use such expensive ointment? Why did she dry them with her hair?

Why did Jesus answer Judas as He did? Why did He mention the poor? What was the main point of His response?

What Is the Place of Money in Your Life?

There are four positions that people hold toward money and material gain.

1. Idolatry

For some people, money becomes central to their lives. They worship money, which means that they devote most of their time, energy, and attention to its gain and use. They regard money as the key to having power and prestige. Ask yourself these questions:

How much time do I spend thinking about my financial life each day? In comparison, how much time do I spend in God's Word or meditating upon it?

How much time do I spend working or shopping in a week? Be sure to include trips to the ATM, discussions about budgets or spending plans, and the time spent paying bills and balancing your checking account. In comparison, how much time do you spend in prayer, reading your Bible, or participating in church-related activities?

Am I more likely to discuss a hot stock tip, the cost of an item, a new business opportunity—or an insight into God's Word, the major truths of last Sunday's sermon, or a way in which the Holy Spirit helped me during the day?

You may say that you trust God in every area of your life, but then conduct business transactions, make purchases and investments, and enter into money-making opportunities without ever asking God's opinion or seeking His wisdom. An idol can be anything that you place above God in your heart and mind. It is anything that you trust more than you trust God, anything that you love more than the things of God. When you leave God out of your financial life, you are in grave danger of making money your idol.

> Do you not know that the unrighteous will not inherit the kingdom of God? Do not be deceived. Neither fornicators, nor idolaters, nor adulterers, nor homosexuals, nor sodomites, nor thieves, nor covetous, nor drunkards, nor revilers, nor extortioners will inherit the kingdom of God.

> —1 Corinthians 6:9–10

 Why does Paul list covetousness right beside these other sins? What does this suggest about God's view of materialism?

 Why does Paul warn us not to be deceived concerning these things? In what ways might a person deceive himself about making money an idol?

15

2. Envy

A second position that people often have toward money is the sin of envy. They aren't likely to admit that they are envious. They are more likely to say, "I'm poor but honest." The assumption underlying that statement is that those who are rich aren't honest.

People who hold this position assume that those who have money must have gained it through illegal or ungodly means. They believe that the rich are rich because they are selfish and they refuse to give to the poor what "rightfully" belongs to the poor. People often hold this position because they feel cheated in some way. They think that the rich have what they have because they have taken it from people who don't have as much.

That is rarely the case. Most people with great wealth in our nation have it because they have worked hard, have invested their time and money astutely, or have inherited their money (which means that someone before them worked hard and invested time and money wisely). Furthermore, the rich do not owe the poor anything that the poor are capable of earning for themselves.

I don't want you to misunderstand what I am saying. We are called upon very clearly in the Bible to take care of the poor and to provide for them, but the poor are always assumed in the Scriptures to be those who are incapable of taking care of themselves. The poor are nearly always defined as widows and orphans—those who do not have a designated provider within a family structure. "The poor" is not a classification according to financial status—in other words, those who fall below the poverty line. "The poor" in the Bible refers to someone who is unable to meet his or her needs. In plain, modern-day language, we are to help *those who have nobody else to help them*, which may very well include abandoned children, older people, desperately sick or injured people, or others who are alone and in dire need.

The Bible clearly states that able-bodied and capable people are to work and provide for their own needs. Furthermore, the Bible speaks very strongly against these things:

- Procrastination

- Laziness

- Slothfulness

The Bible teaches that people have a responsibility to do the utmost that they can for themselves. And then after they have done all that they are capable of doing, the community at large is to provide what still remains as a need. This provision is to come from all who have any excess in their lives.

At no place in the Scriptures do we find the Lord commanding us to take on freeloaders or to pay the entire bill for those who are capable of earning at least part of their way. The poor are given no right to expect the rich to pay any portion of the bills that they can pay for themselves. We are to help people improve their lot in life and to help them climb the economic ladder, but at no time does God command us to become the sole source of provision for lazy, unproductive, and slothful people.

It is not only the destitute and poor who can feel envious of the wealth of others. Envious people may very well have a great deal, but they don't have what they think they should have or what they think they deserve. Some people who have a great deal are sorely dissatisfied with their lot in life. They feel it unfair if someone else has more than they have. In the Bible, people who are envious of the things that others have are called *covetous*.

You shall not covet your neighbor's house; you shall not covet your neighbor's wife, nor his male servant, nor his female servant, nor his ox, nor his donkey, nor anything that is your neighbor's.

—Exodus 20:17

∽ What does it mean to covet? Give specific examples.

∽ In what ways do people try to disguise their coveting? How do people justify their coveting by calling it something different?

3. Greed

Both idolatry and envy can easily result in greed. Greed is an insatiable desire for more. It is often related to money and material goods, although it can be exhibited toward other desires as well. People with great wealth, people with no wealth, and people of all economic levels in between are equally prone to greed, for greed is a state of the heart.

The greedy person says, "I deserve more than I have simply because I want more." Such a person rarely acknowledges that he has responsibility for his current lot in life. Greedy people tend to blame others for their lack. At the core of greed are a refusal to take personal responsibility and a refusal to trust God. The greedy person does not truly believe that God will take care of him, that God loves him, or that God has blessed him. He tends to regard God as stingy and unfair.

The greedy person believes that if God truly loved him, He would give him everything that he desires. The greedy person wants God to prove His love through a shower of material blessings. Two main problems exist, however: (1) the greedy person denies that God might express His love in any other terms than the material, and (2) there is no end to what the greedy heart desires.

The greedy person does not allow God to fill the void that he feels in his heart with God's presence. He wants things to fill the void. Money and possessions can never fill that void; therefore, the voracious hunger of greed is never satisfied. The greedy person wants more, more, more of everything—that is, except God. The Bible has much to say about the greedy person—none of it good. Do not conclude too quickly that you are free of all greed in your life. You are prone to greed to the degree that you fail to trust God completely to meet all your needs—spiritual, mental, emotional, physical, or material.

But they lie in wait for their own blood, They lurk secretly for their own lives. So are the ways of everyone who is greedy for gain; It takes away the life of its owners.

—Proverbs 1:18–19

❧ The picture in these verses is of a person who is hunting birds. In what ways is a greedy person similar to a man who sets a snare for a bird?

❧ How does greed take away a person's life? Give examples.

4. Neutrality

The fourth position that we can take toward money is to recognize that money is neutral. This is the position that is wise. A twenty-dollar bill can be used to buy a bottle of booze, which can help lead to a ruined life, or to buy a Bible for a person who doesn't know the Lord, which can help lead to eternal life. The twenty-dollar bill by itself has no morality associated with it. In other words, it's the attitude toward our money and what we do with it that counts.

God is far more concerned about your attitudes and desires toward money than He is about your current bank statement. He is far more concerned about how you spend your money and allocate your resources than with your starting or ending balance.

> Do not be deceived, God is not mocked; for whatever a man sows, that he will also reap. For he who sows to his flesh will of the flesh reap corruption, but he who sows to the Spirit will of the Spirit reap everlasting life.

> —Galatians 6:7–8

What does it mean to sow to the flesh? Give specific examples.

What does it mean to sow to the spirit? Give specific examples.

⌦ In what ways does a person "reap corruption" by sowing to the flesh? How does one reap everlasting life by sowing to the spirit?

⌦ Today and Tomorrow ⌦

TODAY: THE LORD WANTS ME TO TAKE A NEUTRAL ATTITUDE TOWARD MONEY, USING IT AS A TOOL FOR HIS KINGDOM.

TOMORROW: I WILL ASK THE LORD TO REVEAL TO ME WHETHER I HAVE A SPIRIT OF GREED OR ENVY.

LESSON 3

Money and Your Faith

--- ✺ **In This Lesson** ✺ ---

LEARNING: WHAT IS THE DIFFERENCE BETWEEN RICHES AND PROSPERITY?

GROWING: WHAT SHOULD BE MY PRIMARY FOCUS IN LIFE?

There is a strong correlation between money and your spiritual life. The way that you handle money indicates a great deal about your relationship with God. Godliness has a dimension of concern about the handling of the material world, including stewardship of nature. God is concerned about His material creation, and you are to be concerned about the material world. For the godly, however, the foremost concern in life is to be placed on spiritual growth and development.

The ungodly are careless with the material and natural world, although they spend most of their time thinking about ways to use it to make money. They have virtually no concern for nourishing their spiritual nature.

In Revelation we see that a sign of the end times is an overemphasis on riches and a total preoccupation with material goods. It is a graphic manifestation of how the ungodly have run their course and have spent their all on material pursuits:

The kings of the earth who committed fornication and lived luxuriously with [the queen of Babylon] will weep and lament for her, when they see the smoke of her burning, standing at a distance for fear of her torment, saying, "Alas, alas, that great city Babylon, that mighty city! For in one hour your judgment has come." And the merchants of the earth will weep and mourn over her, for no one buys their merchandise anymore: merchandise of gold and silver, precious stones and pearls, fine linen and purple, silk and scarlet, every kind of citron wood, every kind of object of ivory, every kind of object of most precious wood, bronze, iron, and marble; and cinnamon and incense, fragrant oil and frankincense, wine and oil, fine flour and wheat, cattle and sheep, horses and chariots, and bodies and souls of men. The fruit that your soul longed for has gone from you, and all the things which are rich and splendid have gone from you, and you shall find them no more at all. The merchants of these things, who became rich by her, will stand at a distance for fear of her torment, weeping and wailing, and saying, "Alas, alas, that great city that was clothed in fine linen, purple, and scarlet, and adorned with gold and precious stones and pearls! For in one hour such great riches came to nothing." Every shipmaster, all who travel by ship, sailors, and as many as trade on the sea, stood at a distance and cried out when they saw the smoke of her burning, saying, "What is like this great city?" They threw dust on their heads and cried out, weeping and wailing, and saying, "Alas, alas, that great city, in which all who had ships on the sea became rich by her wealth! For in one hour she is made desolate."

—Revelation 18:9–19

What a picture we have in this passage! The leaders, the merchants, the sailors, and the traders are all devastated at their loss of wealth.

There is no mention of the state of their souls. They have completely sacrificed their faith at the altar of wealth. Their entire pursuit in life has turned to a pursuit of material gain; there is no mention of spiritual gain or loss. They are ungodly to their core.

🕮 Why are the people of the world grieved by the devastation that has come upon Babylon in these verses? What loss are they mourning?

🕮 Notice the list of things that were bought and sold in Babylon—including the "bodies and souls of men." What does this reveal about the world's value system?

Let me be very clear on this point: a concern about material gain is not in itself ungodly. Rather, a concern for material wealth that chokes out concern for one's spiritual health is ungodly. A life out of balance is destined for failure, not success.

The fact that God wants us to register a balanced concern for material gain is found throughout the Scriptures. The Lord wants us to grow in every area of our lives—to be growing spiritually, emotionally, in friendships and family ties, and in material sustenance—always in balance, but always growing. We are to invest our abilities and assets wisely so that growth is possible. When we completely abandon our potential, refusing to do anything with the gifts that God has given us, God is displeased. He is not displeased that we gain wealth. He is displeased when we gain wealth at the expense of other areas of our lives.

Jesus taught this principle in one of His most famous parables:

> For the kingdom of heaven is like a man traveling to a far country, who called his own servants and delivered his goods to them. And to one he gave five talents, to another two, and to another one, to each according to his own ability; and immediately he went on a journey. Then he who had received the five talents went and traded with them, and made another five talents. And likewise he who had received two gained two more also. But he who had received one went and dug in the ground, and hid his lord's money. After a long time the lord of those servants came and settled accounts with them. So he who had received five talents came and brought five other talents, saying, "Lord, you delivered to me five talents; look, I have gained five more talents besides them." His lord said to him, "Well done, good and faithful servant; you were faithful over a few things, I will make you ruler over many things. Enter into the joy of your lord." He also who had received two talents came and said, "Lord, you delivered to me two talents; look, I have gained two more talents besides them." His lord said to him, "Well done, good and faithful servant; you have been faithful over a few things, I will make you ruler over many things. Enter into the joy of your lord." Then he who had received the one talent came and said, "Lord, I knew you to be a hard man, reaping where you have not sown, and gathering where you have not scattered seed. And I was afraid, and went and hid your talent in the ground. Look, there you have what is yours." But his lord answered and said to him, "You wicked and lazy

servant, you knew that I reap where I have not sown, and gather where I have not scattered seed. So you ought to have deposited my money with the bankers, and at my coming I would have received back my own with interest. Therefore take the talent from him, and give it to him who has ten talents. For to everyone who has, more will be given, and he will have abundance; but from him who does not have, even what he has will be taken away. And cast the unprofitable servant into the outer darkness. There will be weeping and gnashing of teeth."

—Matthew 25:14–30

⌦ The "talent" in this parable is a unit of money, not innate skills or gifts. Why did the Lord focus on money in this parable, rather than on other areas of gift?

⌦ Why did the master in this parable give more responsibility to those who had invested wisely? What does this teach about God's perspective of finances?

⌦ What did the "wicked and lazy" servant do that was wrong? What attitude toward God did he reveal?

Points from the Parable

I want you to notice several things from this parable.

First, all of the initial talents given are from the lord. He gave the talents freely to his servants and wanted them to use them and be blessed in the process. Everything that you have is a gift from God to you. He expects you to use what you have been given and, as you use it, to be blessed.

If you are sitting back today and refusing to use some or all of the talents that God has given to you, you are greatly limiting God's blessing in your life. Furthermore, you are cutting short your joy in life, and you are denying yourself a closer relationship with God.

Notice the repeated phrase, "Enter into the joy of your lord." Jesus was teaching that people who risk their potential and invest what they have are subject to tangible reward, and they are going to experience the pleasure of the Lord. God delights in people who give of themselves and who are willing to trust Him to honor their efforts. Such people are pleasing to God; they give Him joy, and they, in turn, share in that joy. Their relationship with God is exhilarating, loving, and joyful!

Second, each of the servants was given a different amount of talents. One servant was given five talents, another two talents, and another one talent. Jesus said that was "according to his own ability." There are people who are blessed in unique ways. They have greater capacities for learning, for receiving, for giving, than other people have.

Some people consider this discouraging news. They don't feel that this is fair. But this is life. God knew from the outset that certain people would be more ambitious than others—they would invest themselves more fully, work harder, use their talents more efficiently—and He knew that the end result would be a society in which some people had acquired everything and others nothing. That was one of the reasons that God instituted the year of Jubilee for the children of Israel. Every fifty years, all debts were to be canceled, and those who had submitted themselves to slavery to pay their debts were to be set free. The playing field was made more level so that the nation as a whole could remain in balance.

You could wipe clean the financial slates of every person in our nation today, and within a few years, you would again have wealthy people and poor people. This would not be solely because some are five-talent and two-talent people and others are one-talent people. Some people are willing to invest themselves—to give of who they are and what they have—and others are not. Some five-talent people don't use their talents. Some two-talent people don't give of themselves or develop their potential. Some one-talent people are doing all they can and giving all they can. The issue is not the amount of talents that people have been given, but what they are doing with them. Jesus taught:

> He who is faithful in what is least is faithful also in much; and he who is unjust in what is least is unjust also in much. Therefore if you have not been faithful in the unrighteous mammon, who will commit to your trust the true riches? And if you have not been faithful in what is another man's, who will give you what is your own?
>
> —Luke 16:10–12

You must never lose sight of the fact that in this story every servant was given something. You have a gift from God. You have spiritual gifts, mental capabilities, physical attributes, and material possessions. The fact that you have them is not what matters. The important thing is this: What are you doing with what you have been given?

∼ What does it mean to be "faithful in what is least"? Whom do you know that is faithful in small things?

∼ What does it mean to be "faithful in the unrighteous mammon"? What is a faithful use of money?

∼ Why would God refuse to entrust someone with "true riches" if he has been unfaithful with material riches?

Third, the servant who refused to risk investing his one talent did so out of fear. Fear is the number one obstacle that keeps people from giving of themselves. These fears are not rooted in an external reality; they are fears of the mind and heart:

∼ A fear of failure

∼ A fear of disappointment—either of disappointing others or disappointing ourselves

🔊 A fear of what others will say about us—a fear of losing face or diminishing our reputation

🔊 A fear of loss and of being a lesser person

The servant in Jesus' parable said that he was afraid of his master's displeasure. Some people are afraid that God will punish them for making a mistake, so they refuse to take any risks with their faith. Fear doesn't keep us from failure—fear causes failure. The lord in this parable punished the unprofitable servant, not for failing to succeed, but for failing to try! That's a very important point related to faith.

God does not require that we be successful. He does not punish us for failing to succeed. But He is very disappointed when we fail to give our best and fail to make the attempt. When a person refuses to take a risk because he is fearful, he is saying these things about his relationship with God:

🔊 "I don't trust God to help me accomplish this or to direct me wisely so that I can succeed."

🔊 "I don't trust God to reward my effort, only punish my failure."

Can you see how integral faith is to the management of your material goods and your many talents? Either you trust God to help you, teach you, and lead you to the place where He will reward you, or you don't. Either you believe that God is on your side and desires to help you fulfill your God-given potential and reap the blessings that He has prepared for you, or you believe that God is against you and is waiting in the shadows to find an excuse to undermine you or defeat you.

Ultimately, you must admit to yourself and to God: "I trust You enough to obey Your Word, do Your will, commit myself to You completely, and operate in financial stewardship the way that You have prescribed"—or, "I don't trust You, and therefore I will live my life according to my own wits and will." Either you trust God with all of your life, or you don't.

> You will keep him in perfect peace, Whose mind is stayed on You, Because he trusts in You. Trust in the Lord forever, For in Yah, the Lord, is everlasting strength.
>
> —Isaiah 26:3–4

How might a lack of peace cause you to use money foolishly? How can a deep trust in God help you use money more wisely?

What does it mean to have your mind stayed on God? How is this done, in practical terms?

Prosperity vs. Riches

In our discussion of money and faith, we need to remind ourselves that prosperity and riches are two different things. The difference is summarized below:

Prosperity	Riches
Having all you need and enjoying it	Accumulating money & goods
Being fruitful	
Growing	
All areas of life in balance	
Specific to God's plan for you	

Prosperity includes material gain but is not limited to it. It includes balanced growth and multiplication in all areas of life. The accumulation of wealth is something that you can do without God. You can acquire worldly goods and leave God out of the process. You only need to look around at our world today to see that many people are doing just this.

But you cannot be prosperous without God. You cannot have a fully balanced, fruitful, and joyful life without God. To be truly prosperous, you must be spiritually prosperous—your faith and relationship with God must be growing and fruitful. That can't happen apart from God.

Both rich people and poor people are miserable without God. But prosperous people are joyful, productive, and enthusiastic people, because prosperous people are growing. They have a sense of accomplishment. They are bearing good fruit. They have balanced lives and therefore have a sense of fulfillment and satisfaction.

Both rich people and poor people are prone to jealousy of the wealth of others because they are never satisfied. They regard the possessions of others as belonging rightfully to them. In comparison, prosperous people rejoice at the prosperity of others. They are delighted when others are fruitful and growing because they know that there is no limit to what God can do in a person's life.

Rich people trust only themselves. Prosperous people trust God to show them the ways to be fruitful, to grow, to stay balanced, and to know and do God's will. It takes no faith in God to become rich. It takes faith in God to become prosperous.

> He who trusts in his riches will fall, But the righteous will flourish like foliage.

> —Proverbs 11:28

✍ What is the difference between trusting in one's riches and trusting God for your wealth?

✍ How does a righteous person treat money and possessions? In what ways do the righteous "flourish like foliage"? Give examples.

Prosperity has a lasting, eternal quality. Riches can be wiped away in a day—or in an hour as we read from Revelation earlier in this lesson. Prosperity lasts. Even during times of temporary loss, even during slow times or lulls in one area of life, the person who desires God's prosperity and is living according to God's principles for prosperity has a deep, abiding sense of the Lord's presence, provision, and pleasure.

The person who desires to be prosperous lives in such a way that the promises of God are available to him. The person who seeks only riches is someone to whom the fullness of God's promises does not apply. The person who strives to be rich limits himself to living by the "flesh," which is a scriptural way of saying that a person is limiting himself solely to his capabilities as a human being. The person who pursues prosperity avails himself of God's blessings. He is not limited to what he can do as a person. He is connecting his life to the unlimited God, and there is no limit to the amount of growth and blessing that he might enjoy.

The servants in the parable doubled their investments, but when their lord rewarded them, he said that he would make them rulers over "many things." The message is that there is no end to God's ability to bless people or to cause them to be filled with His goodness. The prophet Jeremiah painted a vivid picture of this:

> Thus says the LORD: "Cursed is the man who trusts in man And makes flesh his strength, Whose heart departs from the LORD. For he shall be like a shrub in the desert, And shall not see when good comes, But shall inhabit the parched places in the wilderness, In a salt land which is not inhabited.
>
> Blessed is the man who trusts in the LORD, And whose hope is the LORD. For he shall be like a tree planted by the waters, Which spreads out its roots by the river, And will not fear when heat comes; But its leaf will be green, And will not be anxious in the year of drought, Nor will cease from yielding fruit."
>
> —Jeremiah 17:5–8

God's desire for you is prosperity. He wants you to be a whole person, balanced and growing and fruitful and fulfilling His plan and purpose for your life. You must ask yourself: *What is my desire? How am I acting on it?*

What does it mean to make flesh your strength? Give specific examples.

What is the hope of the person who desires riches? What is the hope of the person who pursues real prosperity? Which person is like the tree planted by water?

❧ Today and Tomorrow ❧

TODAY: THE LORD WANTS ME TO PROSPER IN ALL AREAS OF MY LIFE—INCLUDING THE SPIRITUAL.

TOMORROW: I WILL ASK THE LORD TO TEACH ME WHAT IT MEANS TO BE TRULY PROSPEROUS IN HIS EYES.

LESSON 4

The Source of Your Prosperity

ꕔ **In This Lesson** ꕔ

LEARNING: WHAT IS THE DIFFERENCE BETWEEN NEEDS AND DESIRES?

GROWING: WHAT MUST I DO FIRST TO RECEIVE GOD'S PROVISIONS?

The Bible is filled from cover to cover with the goodness of God. Our heavenly Father is always giving, always loving, always generous toward His children. In Genesis, He gives the man and woman a perfect Garden of Eden. In Revelation, we read about our ultimate home, a perfect and eternal heaven. In all the books in between, we read how God delighted in blessing His people. At the outset of the New Testament, we read how God sent His Son, Jesus Christ, as His ultimate gift of blessing to us.

God is the Source of all you need. He is the Author of the whole-life, eternal-life prosperity plan. The sovereignty of God over all material wealth is stated clearly in 1 Chronicles. These words of King David also reflect the attitude that we should have toward God's provision:

> Therefore David blessed the LORD before all the assembly; and David said:

> "Blessed are You, LORD God of Israel, our Father, forever and ever.

Yours, O LORD, is the greatness,
The power and the glory,
The victory and the majesty;
For all that is in heaven and in earth is Yours;
Yours is the kingdom, O LORD,
And You are exalted as head over all.
Both riches and honor come from You,
And You reign over all.
In Your hand is power and might;
In Your hand it is to make great
And to give strength to all.
Now therefore, our God,
We thank You
And praise Your glorious name.
But who am I, and who are my people,
That we should be able to offer so willingly as this?
For all things come from You,
And of Your own we have given You."

—1 Chronicles 29:10–14

If we were to summarize David's statement in three short sentences, we might say:

1. The Lord is the owner of everything.

2. The Lord gives generously to His people.

3. We do well to give Him thanks and praise for what He has given us.

Jesus certainly agreed with this when He taught His disciples to conclude their times of prayer by saying, "For Yours is the kingdom and the power and the glory forever. Amen" (Matt. 6:13). God owns everything, has all authority to dispense with it as He chooses, and is worthy of all praise for what He does. And let it be so!

David reflected about going up to the house of the Lord in Jerusalem:

> Pray for the peace of Jerusalem:
> "May they prosper who love you.
> Peace be within your walls,
> Prosperity within your palaces."

—Psalm 122:6–7

He gave us a prayer that we can pray for all Christians, a prayer that is totally in line with God's will for His people. The Scriptures are filled with verses that tell us of God's goodness, His inexhaustible resources, and His desire to make His people prosper. God's desire for you is prosperity—that you might have all that you need and the capacity to enjoy it.

> Oh, taste and see that the LORD is good; Blessed is the man who trusts in Him! Oh, fear the LORD, you His saints! There is no want to those who fear Him. The young lions lack and suffer hunger; But those who seek the LORD shall not lack any good thing.

—Psalm 34:8–10

✍ Why does the Psalmist tell us to "taste and see" the Lord's goodness?

39

🐟 Why does he mention young lions? How do lions meet their own needs? How is this different from the person who trusts God?

🐟 Why does the Psalmist say that those who seek the Lord shall not lack any good thing? Why does he not say "shall not lack anything"? What does this suggest about God's provision?

When you limit yourself to your own ability and resources, you find that you run out of both ability and resources very quickly. When you focus your faith on what God can do for you, you confront an infinite supply that cannot be measured and cannot be depleted. God's resources are 100 percent inflation-proof, depression-proof, and recession-proof. The very nature of God gives you assurance of His abundant provision:

🐟 Omniscient—God knows your need. He knows it even better than you do and before you do.

🐟 Omnipotent—God has all power to supply what you need.

🐟 Omnipresent—God is at work even now to meet your needs.

You have the character of God as your assurance that He is going to provide for you, and you also have testimony of God's past performance in providing for His people. The Scriptures repeatedly point to Him as a faithful Source:

He made a way for His people to cross the Red Sea and escape from their enemies.

He provided manna for the people to eat in the wilderness.

He caused water to gush forth from a rock to quench His people's thirst.

He gave His commandments to the people when they were without moral fiber.

He healed His people when they were struck by poisonous snakes.

His provision for His people was complete, in every area of their lives.

> Every good gift and every perfect gift is from above, and comes down from the Father of lights, with whom there is no variation or shadow of turning.

> —James 1:17

What are some of the good and perfect gifts that the Lord has given you?

◈ What does it mean that there is "no variation or shadow of turning" in God's character? What does this suggest concerning God's gifts for the future?

◈ By inference, where do bad gifts and imperfect gifts come from? What does this suggest about times when the Lord does *not* provide what we desire?

God's Provision for All Your Need

In Philippians 4:19, God promises to supply all your need. You have very specific needs—emotional, physical, material, mental, and spiritual. All your needs must be met if you are to carry out the complete life plan that God has ordained for you.

You must not compare your needs to those of others. Another person may have a different level of need because God has asked him to do something that requires more resources of one type or another. You can be assured that God will always meet all of your needs. Jesus spoke of God's promise to supply all your needs:

Therefore I say to you, do not worry about your life, what you will eat or what you will drink; nor about your body, what you will put on. Is not life more than food and the body more than clothing? Look at the birds of the air, for they neither sow nor reap nor gather into barns; yet your heavenly Father feeds them. Are you not of more value than they? Which of you by worrying can add one cubit to his stature? So why do you worry about clothing? Consider the lilies of the field, how they grow: they neither toil nor spin; and yet I say to you that even Solomon in all his glory was not arrayed like one of these. Now if God so clothes the grass of the field, which today is, and tomorrow is thrown into the oven, will He not much more clothe you, O you of little faith? Therefore do not worry, saying, "What shall we eat?" or "What shall we drink?" or "What shall we wear?" For after all these things the Gentiles seek. For your heavenly Father knows that you need all these things. But seek first the kingdom of God and His righteousness, and all these things shall be added to you.

Matthew 6:25–33

Note that the Lord encourages you to seek first the things that are spiritual, the things that pertain to the kingdom of God and His righteousness. When you do that, the Lord adds everything else to your life. He gives you a total provision for a whole life. That's prosperity!

In what ways is life more than food? The body more than clothing? What other needs are there besides food and clothes?

What is the kingdom of God? What does it mean to seek it first? How is this done, in practical terms?

Many people have confessed to me that they believe that God is the Source of all things and He supplies abundantly for His people, but they have difficulty believing that God will provide for *them* personally. They believe in the general principle and the broad truth that God takes care of His people, but they admit to doubts and questions about whether God will provide what they need. Let's turn our attention to some areas that are related to this broader concern about whether God will meet personal needs.

Needs and Desires

A *need* is something that you must have in order to stay alive and carry out God's will for your life. Unless your needs are met, you are unable to survive or fulfill the destiny that God has ordained for you. A *desire* is something that might be considered a pleasantry or a nicety. It's fun to have—enjoyable, satisfying, delightful.

Some people believe that God provides only for our bare-essential needs. They question whether what they are requesting is truly a need, believing that, if they ask for anything that they desire but don't need, God will not grant it. But that isn't the message of the Bible. God's provision for us is one of abundance. Jesus taught:

> The thief [the devil] does not come except to steal, and to kill, and to destroy. I have come that they may have life, and that they may have it more abundantly.

—John 10:10

> Give, and it will be given to you: good measure, pressed down, shaken together, and running over will be put into your bosom.

—Luke 6:38

God's desire for you is abundance—a pressed-down, shaken-together, and running-over prosperity. Don't be afraid to ask God for what you desire as well as what you need.

As a parent and a grandfather, I take great joy in giving things to my children and grandchildren. It isn't a matter of whether they need these things. I certainly see to it first and foremost that their basic needs are met. But I have joy in giving them things that are beyond their needs— in giving them the desires of their hearts. The heavenly Father has this same generosity of spirit toward you. He is not a stingy, cheap, or begrudging God. God's only constraints regarding the desires of your heart are that they do not keep you from fulfilling His plan for you on the earth, and that they are things that will benefit you and not cause you harm.

∽ What does it mean to have life more abundantly? What aspects of life make it more abundant? How are such things attained?

∽ Picture a container of flour that is "pressed down, shaken together, and running over". What does this picture teach about God's generosity toward His children?

∽ What is required of us first in order to receive such an abundant blessing?

✒ Repeated Requests ✒

Some people believe that God will not supply their needs, much less grant their desires, unless they meet certain requirements—one of which being that they ask God repeatedly and frequently for what they need. There is no need to plead or beg God for what you need. If that were the case, God would be no better than a miserly human being! God knows what you need. He already desires to meet your needs before you ask Him. So do ask, but don't feel that you must ask repeatedly.

✒ Preconditions ✒

God asks certain things of you if you are to receive His generosity. I believe that these commandments are intended to keep you looking to God so that you are fully capable of receiving from Him and then wisely using the abundance that He pours out on you. Obedience to God's plan keeps you disciplined.

1. *God requires that we keep His commandments*. Deuteronomy 28 is a wonderful example of this. The entire chapter will help you understand God's provision, but let me focus on just this one passage:

> If you diligently obey the voice of the LORD your God, to observe carefully all His commandments which I command you today, that the LORD your God will set you high above all nations of the earth. And all these blessings shall come upon you and overtake you, because you obey the voice of the Lord your God.... The LORD will grant you plenty of goods, in the fruit of your body, in the increase of your livestock, and in the produce of your ground, in the land of which the LORD swore to your fathers to give you. The LORD will open to you His good treasure, the heavens, to give the rain to your land in its season, and to bless all the work of your hand. You shall lend to many

nations, but you shall not borrow. And the LORD will make you the head and not the tail; you shall be above only, and not be beneath, if you heed the commandments of the LORD your God, which I command you today, and are careful to observe them. So you shall not turn aside from any of the words which I command you this day, to the right or the left, to go after other gods to serve them.

—Deuteronomy 28:1–2, 11–14

Note these words and phrases in the passage: "plenty of goods," "increase," "good treasure," "bless," and "head and not the tail." Note also that God's children are to have enough to lend to others, and they will have no necessity to borrow. When you keep God's commandments and live according to His principles, you are in a position to enjoy this kind of prosperity.

2. God also requires that you be generous and giving to others. Note the balance in 1 Timothy:

Command those who are rich in this present age not to be haughty, nor to trust in uncertain riches but in the living God, who gives us richly all things to enjoy. Let them do good, that they be rich in good works, ready to give, willing to share, storing up for themselves a good foundation for the time to come, that they may lay hold on eternal life.

God trusts the generous person with more. He knows you will use what He gives you to bless others. And still, you will never suffer a deficit or loss because you will always be receiving an overflowing supply in return!

—1 Timothy 6:17–19

3. God requires that you believe in Him and His Word. If you don't believe that God is going to supply all your need or grant you the desire of your heart, you aren't going to be looking for those things to arrive. In other words, you won't be ready for your blessing when it shows up. Refer back to 2 Chronicles 20:20. Believing that God will meet your needs and grant your desires is an important prerequisite to having your needs met and your desires granted.

If you are having difficulty believing that God will meet your personal needs, ask God to help you believe. Ask the Lord to help you with your attitude and to help you to trust Him more. That is a cry from the heart that God delights in answering. God longs to hear His people express their dependency on Him and to ask Him for help in trusting Him more.

~ In what ways can riches make a person "haughty"?

~ Notice in the 1 Timothy passage above that Paul does not instruct the rich to become poor. What *does* he instruct them to do? How are these things accomplished?

❧ Other Preconditions? ❧

There is *no* precondition to achieve sainthood before God will bless you. There is *no* precondition for certain rituals to be completed or for a certain number of hours to be spent in prayer and fasting for a need to be answered. There is no checklist or point system that God uses in meting out rewards to His people. God desires that you trust Him to meet your needs, and trust is a matter of faith, not works. God desires that you give of what you have to bless others, and this is a matter of trusting God, not a matter of working your way to deserve rewards.

God's provision for you is out of His heart. It is motivated entirely by His unending love for you. It is not anything that you deserve or accomplish. When you believe in God, keep His commandments, and begin to act with generosity toward others, you will receive blessings from God more fully. God, however, is always in a position to give. He never moves from that position.

❧ A Uniform or Tailored Supply? ❧

Some people erroneously believe that God supplies needs and grants desires uniformly—one provision fits all. That isn't the case. God's supply is always tailored to suit your specific, personal need. Sometimes you don't even know what that need involves. You may see only part of the need or even think that your need lies in one area when it really lies in another. God always supplies the true need. Furthermore, God always supplies your need in the fullness of His timing. He gives what you need so that you might glorify Him and fulfill His purposes in the particular circumstance in which you find yourself.

The apostle Paul thought that his need was for the Lord to remove his "thorn in the flesh." Three times he prayed for the Lord to meet that need. God met Paul's need, but not in the way that Paul envisioned. He

49

made it clear that Paul really needed an awareness of God's grace that was capable of matching any need. (See 2 Cor. 12:7-9.)

God's schedule and timetable don't always match yours, but let me assure you, God is never late in meeting your need. Furthermore, God doesn't react to need. He knows your upcoming need and He has already prepared a provision to meet it. I experienced this in a profound way prior to moving to Atlanta many years ago. I received a sizable gift that was designated for my personal use, and as I prayed about what the Lord might want me to do with it, He revealed that I should hold on to it for a while; His purposes would be revealed in His timing.

Four months later, the Lord directed me to move to Atlanta from Florida. The position in Atlanta did not have a parsonage, so for the first time in my ministry I was required to buy a home. The amount that I had been given four months previously was within one hundred dollars of the total down payment required for me to buy our first house.

What God gives to you He may not give to another person, and vice versa. What God gives you at one time in your life may not be what He gives you in another season. The children of Israel knew this in gathering manna. They were to gather just enough for the day; any excess spoiled. But on the day before the Sabbath, they were to gather two portions. The excess did not spoil, and they had a sufficient supply for two days. No manna was provided on the Sabbath day.

So, too, with God's provision to you. Sometimes He meets the daily need only; at other times He gives you excess to use according to His purposes and plan. At times He calls upon you to rest in Him and to use past provision to meet your current need. (See Ex. 16:15-30.)

And my God shall supply all your need according to His riches in glory by Christ Jesus.

—Philippians 4:19

≈ Why does Paul speak of Christ's "riches in glory"? Why not "riches in material goods"? What does this suggest about God's priorities?

≈ How does this compare with your own priorities?

Your Inability and God's Ability

You may find it useful to develop a chart to remind yourself of God's all-sufficiency in meeting your needs and His loving generosity in granting your desires. Add to this list as you read God's Word regularly.

My Ability to Supply My Needs	God's Ability to Supply My Needs
finite and limited	inexhaustible, infinite, unlimited
inadequate	totally adequate
disappears in famine	exists in famine
constant battle against loss	constant provision in spite of generous giving

Above all, God desires to bless you with an abundance of spiritual gifts. God has "blessed [you] with every spiritual blessing" (Eph. 1:3). Come to your heavenly Father desiring the blessings as your first priority. Come to Him as a child whom He loves. Focus your faith on His love and His desire for you to have everything that you need in this life and in the life to come. Can you dip the ocean dry with a thimble? No, you can never deplete the Source of your prosperity. You can only fail to come to Him and receive all that He has for you.

❧ Today and Tomorrow ☙

TODAY: THE LORD IS MY UNLIMITED SOURCE FOR PROVISION, AND HE WANTS ME TO BE GENEROUS WITH OTHERS.

TOMORROW: I WILL ASK THE LORD TO TEACH ME HOW TO BE A GENEROUS BLESSING TO OTHERS THIS WEEK.

LESSON 5

The Role of Work

─── ❧ **In This Lesson** ❧ ───

LEARNING: IS THERE SOMETHING THAT I'M SUPPOSED TO BE DOING TOWARD PROSPERITY?

GROWING: WHAT SHOULD I DO IF I HATE MY JOB?

If you want greater prosperity in your life, there are two main things that you need to do:

First, ask God to enlarge your faith. Receiving His blessing is directly related to your ability to believe God, to listen to His directions, and to act upon what He says to do.

Second, ask God to enlarge your usefulness—your capacity and ability to work. Most people don't equate greater prosperity with greater work. As a society, we want more money and less work. That, however, is not a scriptural principle. Work is God's divine plan to prosper us.

❧ What is your attitude toward work? Toward your job? Toward other responsibilities and chores?

∾ What motivates you in your career or other responsibilities? What jobs would you be willing to do even if you weren't paid?

God's Plan for Work

God commands that we work. Even in giving Adam and Eve a perfect garden to call their home, God required them to "subdue" the earth—to dress and keep the garden, to have dominion over the other creatures, and to gather from creation the food that they needed. God created Adam and Eve to participate fully in the ongoing management of His creation, and that required exertion of effort and completion of tasks. Work is a part of our identity as human beings. Proverbs tells us plainly:

> Wealth gained by dishonesty will be diminished,
> But he who gathers by labor will increase.
>
> —Proverbs 13:11

God commends our labor, and He chastises those who don't work. One of the most quoted passages of the Bible is Proverbs 31:10–31, a passage about the "virtuous wife." This woman is held out as a model to follow. Note how many of the attributes ascribed to her relate to work.

> Her worth is far above rubies.
> The heart of her husband safely trusts her;
> So he will have no lack of gain.
> She does him good and not evil
> All the days of her life.

She seeks wool and flax,
And willingly works with her hands.
She is like the merchant ships,
She brings her food from afar.
She also rises while it is yet night,
And provides food for her household,
And a portion for her maidservants.
She considers a field and buys it;
From her profits she plants a vineyard.
She girds herself with strength,
And strengthens her arms.
She perceives that her merchandise is good,
And her lamp does not go out by night.
She stretches out her hands to the distaff,
And her hand holds the spindle.
She extends her hand to the poor,
Yes, she reaches out her hands to the needy.
She is not afraid of snow for her household,
For all her household is clothed with scarlet.
She makes tapestry for herself;
Her clothing is fine linen and purple.
Her husband is known in the gates,
When he sits among the elders of the land.
She makes linen garments and sells them,
And supplies sashes for the merchants.
Strength and honor are her clothing;
She shall rejoice in time to come.
She opens her mouth with wisdom,
And on her tongue is the law of kindness.
She watches over the ways of her household;
And does not eat the bread of idleness.
Her children rise up and call her blessed;
Her husband also, and he praises her:

"Many daughters have done well,
But you excel them all."
Charm is deceitful and beauty is passing,
But a woman who fears the LORD, she shall be praised.
Give her of the fruit of her hands,
And let her own works praise her in the gates.

🔖 In the verses above, underline all the passages that are about work—including charitable work and work on behalf of her family, and the wise management of resources.

🔖 Which of those passages is reflected in your life? Which areas do you need to strengthen?

Some people think that, if they just believe hard enough in God's ability to meet their needs, they will not have to work to provide for their sustenance. Some of the believers in the early church at Thessalonica were like that. They were so intent on believing in the Lord's soon return that they spent their days going from house to house to stir up others in their belief. Paul had strong words for them and for any person today who is lazy or who mooches off others.

Paul had a strong tradition in his life of working for his keep as a tent maker (or leather worker). He did this as an example to anyone who might think that a person engaged in ministry had a right to be lazy. In God's eyes, all people need to employ all of their talents to the best of their ability and with a maximum amount of energy.

God requires that we work, and simultaneously He leads others to compensate us for our work. In 1 Thessalonians 4:10–12 above, note that Paul speaks to the Thessalonians because he desires that they "increase more and more." The virtuous woman of Proverbs 31 is to be praised and to receive rewards. A marvelous example of compensation for good work is found in the life of Joseph, the eleventh son of Jacob. Joseph was taken by Ishmaelites down into Egypt, where an officer of Pharaoh named Potiphar bought him as a slave. Even though Joseph was a slave:

> the LORD was with Joseph, and he was a successful man; and he was in the house of his master the Egyptian. And his master saw that the LORD was with him and that the LORD made all he did to prosper in his hand. So Joseph found favor in his sight, and served him. Then he made him overseer of his house, and all that he had he put under his authority. So it was, from the time that he had made him overseer of his house and all that he had, that the LORD blessed the Egyptian's house for Joseph's sake; and the blessing of the LORD was on all that he had in the house and in the field. Thus he left all that he had in Joseph's hand.
>
> —Genesis 39:2–6

Joseph became overseer of the estate of a prominent Egyptian, which meant that Joseph had the full run of it. He lived well, ate well, and dressed well. He had all of his material needs met because the Lord caused Potiphar to deal with him favorably. If you are giving your best effort and are trusting God to give you wisdom in all of your work endeavors, watch for the ways in which the Lord will cause others to bless you.

Note also that the Egyptian was blessed in return. He had no worries or concerns with Joseph managing his household. Joseph had proven himself worthy of his trust. You must give maximum effort and do well in your work, and you must be trustworthy to those who supervise you.

The day came, however, when Joseph was falsely accused by Potiphar's wife, and Potiphar had Joseph placed in prison. (Even then, Potiphar was acting with kindness to Joseph; he could have had Joseph killed.) While Joseph was in prison, the Lord again brought him into favor:

> But the LORD was with Joseph and showed him mercy, and He gave him favor in the sight of the keeper of the prison. And the keeper of the prison committed to Joseph's hand all the prisoners who were in the prison; whatever they did there, it was his doing. The keeper of the prison did not look into anything that was under Joseph's authority, because the LORD was with him; and whatever he did, the LORD made it prosper.
>
> —Genesis 39:21–23

In the end, Joseph was released from prison. He had trusted God with his life, he had been trustworthy in every circumstance, and he had done such good work in the past that the Lord allowed him to become prime minister of the land, second in command to Pharaoh. Joseph instituted a plan that allowed Egypt to enjoy prosperity in a time of great famine. The famine was severe in Egypt and surrounding countries, yet Egypt had enough grain in storage that people from other countries came for help.

Joseph went from prosperity in one situation to prosperity in another. He never stopped trusting God, he never stopped working, and he never stopped being compensated in ways that were far above what could be expected. When we place our faith in God and keep His commandments, including His commands to work, we are counted among the righteous. We will receive God's blessing. David spoke of God's provision to His people:

> I have been young, and now am old;
> Yet I have not seen the righteous forsaken,
> Nor his descendants begging bread.
> He is ever merciful, and lends;
> And his descendants are blessed.
> Depart from evil, and do good;
> And dwell forevermore.
> For the LORD loves justice,
> And does not forsake His saints;
> They are preserved forever,
> But the descendants of the wicked shall be cut off.
> The righteous shall inherit the land,
> And dwell in it forever.

> —Psalm 37:25–29

❧ What is the connection between being merciful and finding prosperity? Between lending to others and being blessed?

❧ Why does the Lord command us to "depart from evil and do good"? What is the connection between that and experiencing God's prosperity?

Our Attitude Toward Work

God wants you to have several attitudes toward work. Some people believe that their attitude toward work is unimportant as long as they produce well and get a job done. Yet your attitude toward your work is vital in God's eyes. Your attitude will motivate you to do more than is required, produce at a quality level that is above the expected, and reap rewards that are greater than you have ever anticipated.

1. Be goal-oriented in your work. Don't approach a job as something that you are doing just to pay your bills. See your job as something that you have set about to achieve. Set goals for yourself that are beyond the minimum goals required by your employer or others in your field. "Making ends meet" is not a goal. Set a goal that requires you to trust God for abilities, wisdom, insights, and the acquisition of skills that you don't presently have. Set your sights higher than a minimal effort.

The apostle Paul certainly had this attitude when it came to his life and ministry. He wrote to the Philippians:

> Not that I have already attained, or am already perfected; but I press on, that I may lay hold of that for which Christ Jesus has also laid hold of me. Brethren, I do not count myself to have apprehended; but one thing I do, forgetting those things which are behind and reaching forward to those things which are ahead, I press toward the goal for the prize of the upward call of God in Christ Jesus.
>
> —Philippians 3:12–14

Paul was "pressing on" even though he was advanced in years and had a long list of accomplishments to his credit. He was still "reaching forward." He was still looking for "the prize of the upward call." Be as productive as you can be. Do all that you know to do, and then trust God to do through you what you cannot do in your own strength.

> Whatever your hand finds to do, do it with your might; for there is no work or device or knowledge or wisdom in the grave where you are going.
>
> —Ecclesiastes 9:10

∼ What work has your hand found to do? Are you doing it with all your might, or with a "good enough" attitude?

∼ Why does Solomon add the warning about the grave? How can it help your work ethics if you remember that you will not live on earth forever?

The Lord soundly condemns laziness and slothfulness in His Word. Laziness is a refusal to put forth energy and effort, while slothfulness is being wasteful or misusing the resources that are made available to you, including the opportunities that God gives you for work. Both laziness and slothfulness begin with attitude:

> ∼ "I don't need to do any more than what I'm doing. Let others do this. I'm going to take my ease."

⮞ "Nobody will know if I take a shortcut or waste this portion. It won't matter if I don't do my best in this instance."

Some of the strongest words in the Bible are against lazy or slothful people. Read this scathing review of the sluggard from Proverbs:

Go to the ant, you sluggard!
Consider her ways and be wise,
Which, having no captain,
Overseer or ruler,
Provides her supplies in the summer,
And gathers her food in the harvest.
How long will you slumber, O sluggard?
When will you rise from your sleep?
A little sleep, a little slumber,
A little folding of the hands to sleep—
So shall your poverty come on you like a prowler,
And your need like an armed man.

—Proverbs 6:6–11

⮞ List the attributes of the ant which are included in these verses. How many of those traits do you have?

⮞ How does a "prowler" come upon his victim? What is it like to face an armed enemy? What do these images suggest about the results of being lazy?

2. Have an intense desire to do your best at whatever you undertake.
Take pride in your work. Produce the very best quality you can. The
Lord does His work with only one standard: perfection. You are a finite
and limited creation, and you can never be perfect. Neither can you do
perfect work all the time. But you can seek to do better than you have
done in the past. You can refuse to settle for a second-class effort or
performance.

When you do your best, you have a sense of fulfillment and of joy. You
have satisfaction that you have been generous in your effort and in
the giving of yourself. And in that, there is reward, both tangible and
intangible.

> He who is slothful in his work is a brother to him who is a great
> destroyer.
>
> —Proverbs 18:9

What is the connection between being slothful and being a
destroyer?

Give practical examples of how a person's sloth can cause
destruction.

3. Have a positive attitude toward your work and toward those with whom you work. It isn't enough that you are productive and do quality work. You also must have an attitude of cooperation with others. Don't judge or condemn your colleagues; don't gossip about them. God will not honor a critical spirit.

Pray for your supervisors, vendors, and associates. Look for ways in which you can share the love of Christ with them. At all times you are to be a witness to the work of Christ in your life, and especially so in the way that you conduct your business affairs.

> Follow peace with all men, and holiness, without which no man shall see the Lord.
>
> —Hebrews 12:14

How does this verse apply to your work situation? Give practical examples.

In what ways is holiness important in your job? How might holiness increase a person's job satisfaction?

4. Be determined, persistent, and patient in your work. Believe that you can do the job that you have set out to do! Don't expect to succeed or get rich in a day. Don't give up in your good efforts. Don't allow impatience to tempt you to do shoddy work or take shortcuts. Stay true to the course that the Lord has set before you, and trust Him to bring you to a satisfying and rewarding end.

Don't be afraid to take reasonable risks in your work and career. Don't let doubt keep you from pursuing your best. God always has more for you if you will only believe for more and trust God to enlarge your capacity to do more.

> Trust in the LORD with all your heart, And lean not on your own understanding; In all your ways acknowledge Him, And He shall direct your paths.
>
> —Proverbs 3:5–6

What does it mean to lean on your own understanding? How is this different from trusting the Lord with all your heart?

What does it mean to acknowledge the Lord "in all your ways"? How is this done, in practical terms?

Ask God today to guide you in your work:

 To give you the job that's best suited to your talents and abilities, a job through which you can fulfill God's purposes for your life

 To send you the colleagues, clients, employees, customers, and vendors that you need

 To give you wisdom in setting policies and procedures related to your work

 To give you strength to do your best, produce the most possible, and achieve all you can

 To help you maintain a high level of quality in all you undertake

 To renew your enthusiasm daily for the jobs and tasks that are set before you

 To honor your efforts from His great storehouse of unlimited supply

If anyone will not work, neither shall he eat. For we hear that there are some who walk among you in a disorderly manner, not working at all, but are busybodies. Now those who are such we command and exhort through our Lord Jesus Christ that they work in quietness and eat their own bread.

—2 Thessalonians 3:10–12

How do you react to Paul's commandment that people who don't work should not be fed by others? What implications does this teaching have to our modern culture?

What is the connection between not working for a living and being a busybody? Being disorderly?

What does it mean to "work in quietness"? Why is this important?

Today and Tomorrow

TODAY: THE LORD WANTS ME TO EARN MY OWN LIVING, AND TO DO IT WITH ALL MY MIGHT.

TOMORROW: I WILL FOCUS MY EFFORTS ON MY WORK THIS WEEK, TO ACHIEVE MY HIGHEST POTENTIAL.

Lesson 6

Deliverance from Debt

⛧ In This Lesson ⛧

LEARNING: HOW MUCH DEBT IS TOO MUCH?

GROWING: HOW CAN I GET OUT OF FINANCIAL BONDAGE?

The Bible leaves no doubt about God's opinion regarding debt. Here are two verses that deal with this subject, which is a painful one for millions of people:

> Owe no one anything except to love one another, for he who loves another has fulfilled the law.

> —Romans 13:8

> The rich rules over the poor,
> And the borrower is servant to the lender.

> —Proverbs 22:7

Our nation has ignored these truths. One in five families in our nation is on the brink of bankruptcy. Millions of people are within sixty days of being homeless or in dire financial need. We have bought into a buy now and pay later philosophy that has been sold to us for decades by advertisers who tempt us to believe that we must have the product which they are selling in order to project an image of worth. We have swallowed a lie, and we are gagging on it. God does not want His people to be in debt. The only thing that we are to owe others is our love, which we are to give freely and in tangible forms. We are to be givers, not borrowers.

The price for indebtedness can be high. In ancient times, the children of Israel lost much of their land and possessions because of debt, and some sold themselves or their children into slavery in order to pay their debts. In Nehemiah 5:3–5 we find a mournful outcry from God's people:

> There were also some who said, "We have mortgaged our lands and vineyards and houses, that we might buy grain because of the famine." There were also those who said, "We have borrowed money for the king's tax on our lands and vineyards. Yet now our flesh is as the flesh of our brethren, our children as their children; and indeed we are forcing our sons and our daughters to be slaves, and some of our daughters have been brought into slavery. It is not in our power to redeem them, for other men have our lands and vineyards."

This same heart's cry is voiced by a widow who came to the prophet Elisha and said, "Your servant my husband is dead, and you know that your servant feared the Lord. And the creditor is coming to take my two sons to be his slaves" (2 Kings 4:1). This woman's husband was one of the prophets who was associated with Elisha; he apparently had died and left his family in debt. The only recourse that seemed available to the woman was to sell her children into slavery to repay what her husband owed.

We may protest, "How horrible! How could a mother sell her children to work off a debt?" And yet that is exactly what we in the United States are doing in strapping our children with a huge national debt. We have gone from being the world's largest creditor nation to debtor status in a matter of only a few decades. What we have done on a national scale we have also done on an individual and family scale. Our children will be forced to pay for our foolishness.

God is so opposed to debt that He doesn't even want His people to be the security for another person's debt—in our language today, that might mean being the cosigner on a loan:

> Do not be one of those who shakes hands in a pledge [signify-
> ing a loan],
> One of those who is surety for debts;
> If you have nothing with which to pay,
> Why should he take away your bed from under you?
>
> —Proverbs 22:26–27

In other words, God doesn't want you to be faced with the possibility of paying another person's debt, a situation that could put your livelihood and possessions into jeopardy—in this case, even your bed!

What is the risk of being a co-signer on someone else's debt? Why does the Bible warn against doing this?

How much debt are you in? What can you do to reduce your debt?

The Relationship of Debt to Faith

Debt has a negative impact upon the spiritual life. Some of the reasons that God is opposed to debt can be discovered when we take a look at the reasons that people get into debt:

People get into debt because they buy things that they can't afford. Credit cards are bad for many people. They are overused and abused. Buying with a credit card is taking out a loan, however short-term it may be. Unless you can manage credit cards wisely, I suggest that you wean yourself away from them completely.

When we buy things that we can't afford, we are saying to God, "I need this more than I need to be free of debt." We make many credit card purchases so that we can bolster self-esteem. We trust in things to give us a sense of identity and well-being rather than trust God for our identity. Furthermore, when we buy on credit, we aren't trusting God to give us the things that we need *in His timing*. We want what we want *now*. God's plan often requires us to wait for certain things so that we are able to use them fully and wisely, and also so that others can benefit from God's gifts to us. Trust God for His timing in the blessings that you receive. James 1:4 states, "Let patience have its perfect work, that you may be perfect and complete, lacking nothing."

People are in debt because they make unwise investments. God promises to give His people insight, answers, and direction. All we need to do is ask Him for these things, and wait until we are assured of His response. James 1:5-6 advises us, "If any of you lacks wisdom, let him ask of God, who gives to all liberally and without reproach, and it will be given to him. But let him ask in faith, with no doubting."

Too few people turn to God to ask His advice about investments and major purchases, such as homes, cars, and other big-ticket items. Oth-

71

ers fail to seek God's advice before they enter into partnerships or business opportunities that require them to sign contracts or make financial commitments. When we ask God for His wisdom, He will give us clear leading about what to avoid and what to pursue. He can see the ending from the beginning, and He knows what will be best for us now and in the future.

People are in debt because they are careless in their purchases, making unwise or unnecessary choices. Much of what we buy we don't need and, in many cases, don't really want six months later. Fashions change, and fads come and go. I am not advocating that we be old-fashioned in our dress or possessions, yet we should always buy quality items that will last. Again, we need to seek God's wisdom.

People are in debt because they lack forethought for the future. I have met Christian people who believe that they are to live in the moment and never have a savings account, much less provide an inheritance for their children. I disagree. The Bible has very positive things to say about inheritance. For example, Isaac blessed Jacob and said to him:

> May God Almighty bless you,
> And make you fruitful and multiply you ...
> That you may inherit the land
> In which you are a stranger,
> Which God gave to Abraham.
>
> —Genesis 28:3–4

> If any of you lacks wisdom, let him ask of God, who gives to all liberally and without reproach, and it will be given to him. But let him ask in faith, with no doubting, for he who doubts is like a wave of the sea driven and tossed by the wind.
>
> —James 1:5–6

🐚 When have you asked the Lord to give you wisdom regarding an important decision? What was the result?

🐚 Why does James add a warning against doubting when praying for wisdom? What might you be tempted to doubt?

Isaac had inherited the land from his father, Abraham, and was handing it down to his son. If either Abraham or Isaac had lived only for himself and for the moment, he would have had no inheritance to pass on. Proverbs 13:22 declares, "A good man leaves an inheritance to his children's children." A person who lacks forethought for the future leaves no inheritance.

In Jesus' parable about the prodigal son and the loving father, we read about a son who squandered his inheritance, becoming so deeply in debt that his only recourse was to hire himself out to work in the hog pens of a faraway country. He was a young man who had no forethought for the future. (See Luke 15:11-32.)

People are in debt because they lose a job or miss work owing to illness or injury. There may be little that you can do to immunize yourself against a job loss, injury, or illness, but if you have saved a portion of your earnings, you are likely to have a financial cushion to see you through hard times. Debt only compounds the pain and emotional trauma that you and your entire family experience when a member of your family is unable to work to help provide for the family's needs. It is easy during such times to fall into depression, doubt, or discouragement. You will be less likely to experience these faith-debilitating emotions if you have financial means to pay your bills until you are able to work again.

It is far easier to *stay* out of debt than to *get* out of debt. Make a decision that you are going to follow God's plan in your finances and that you are not going to fall prey to the alluring messages that tempt you to borrow, buy beyond your means, or spend your money unwisely.

> A good man leaves an inheritance to his children's children,
> But the wealth of the sinner is stored up for the righteous.
>
> —Proverbs 13:22

☙ What inheritance are you putting aside for the next generation?

☙ How does God bless those who are righteous, even beyond their expectations?

How Much Debt Is Too Much?

I don't believe that owing a bill for a few days or weeks is tantamount to debt. Much of our society is based upon thirty-, forty-five-, or sixty-day pay cycles. We are speaking here about the sort of debt that leads to financial bondage. You know that you are in debt when you:

🍃 can't pay bills as they come due.

🍃 start putting off the payment of one bill in order to pay another.

🍃 feel pressure regarding your bills.

🍃 become worried about how you will pay your bills.

🍃 start looking for quick fixes or quick ways out of your debt.

Debt can lead to a host of attitudes that affect your spiritual life negatively.

First, debt creates stress, anxiety, or deep frustration. The person who suffers from these emotions does not have a heart fully turned toward God. Debt can also become a mental preoccupation—your first and last thoughts each day are about whom you owe, how much you owe, and what you can do about what you owe. You are not in a position to hear from God about His priorities for the use of your time and resources. Ultimately, unpaid debt can lead to fear—a deep anxiety that you will never be out of debt. Fear is the opposite of faith.

Second, debt places a strain on family relationships. Money concerns are among the primary causes of family arguments. Mismanagement of money can smother love. Don't allow that to happen in your home! When disagreements interrupt the free flow of loving communication in your home, you are facing a problem that has spiritual dimensions to it.

Third, debt causes you to become resentful of others. Rather than reach out to others, you begin to avoid those you owe and, at times, those who know about your indebtedness. Debt can cause you to distrust those who seem to have no money problems. It can cause you to become envious. These are not godly attitudes.

Fourth, debt hurts the testimony of a Christian. It is difficult to declare to the world that you are trusting God to meet all of your needs when you are deeply in debt. Your credibility is destroyed.

Debt affects your spiritual life in a negative way because debt keeps you from listening totally to God's directives for your daily life. You lose much of your flexibility when you allow yourself to become burdened by debt.

When you are in debt, you must be concerned about the payment of that debt. That concern rightfully becomes a major priority in your life. In the process, you are no longer free to act immediately should God direct you to do so.

> A certain woman of the wives of the sons of the prophets cried out to Elisha, saying, "Your servant my husband is dead, and you know that your servant feared the LORD. And the creditor is coming to take my two sons to be his slaves." So Elisha said to her, "What shall I do for you? Tell me, what do you have in the house?" And she said, "Your maidservant has nothing in the house but a jar of oil." Then he said, "Go, borrow vessels from everywhere, from all your neighbors--empty vessels; do not gather just a few. And when you have come in, you shall shut the door behind you and your sons; then pour it into all those vessels, and set aside the full ones." So she went from him and shut the door behind her and her sons, who brought the vessels to her; and she poured it out. Now it came to pass, when the vessels were full, that she said to her son, "Bring me another vessel." And he said to her, "There is not another vessel." So the oil ceased. Then she came and told the man of God. And he said, "Go, sell the oil and pay your debt; and you and your sons live on the rest."

> —2 Kings 4:1–7

☙ What caused this woman's debt? What resources did she have to pay the debt?

☙ What did the woman do to get out of her trouble? How can her action be applied to your own debt situation?

☙ How did God miraculously provide for her? When have you seen the Lord miraculously provide for someone that you know?

The Obligation to Pay Debts

You may be tempted to walk away from your indebtedness, justifying your action so that you might be free to follow God's call or to place more emphasis on your spiritual life. But walking away from a debt is not Scriptural. Psalm 37:21 states very clearly:

The wicked borrows and does not repay,
But the righteous shows mercy and gives.

We have an obligation to pay our debts, and God will help us pay them if we will turn to Him and trust Him for wisdom. Two effective examples appear in God's Word, and both involve the prophet Elisha. In the first example, the sons of the prophets wanted a larger place to live, so they asked permission of Elisha to go to the river and cut some beams to make a new home for themselves. Elisha granted them permission and also agreed with their request to go along with them to the river.

As one of the men was cutting down a tree, "the iron ax head fell into the water; and he cried out and said, 'Alas, master! For it was borrowed.' " (See 2 Kings 6:1–5.) Iron was a rare commodity to the children of Israel. The Philistines had control over the natural resources needed for making iron tools and chariots. An iron ax head was costly and not easily replaced. The man recognized without hesitation that he had an obligation to restore the ax head, even though it was an accident. It was an obligation that he could not meet.

God gave Elisha power to work a miracle, making the ax head float to the water's surface—and the man's debt was resolved. It is important in this incident to note that the man was not foolish in his actions. He was working honestly and in good faith when the accident happened. God comes to the aid of those who experience debt in this way. Conversely, God does not promise a miracle to absolve us of debt that is accrued because of our sin or foolishness. He will help us get out of debt in these instances, but He does not miraculously restore our loss.

The second miracle we have already touched upon, involving the widow who came to Elisha. Elisha told her to borrow (only temporarily) all the vessels that she could from her friends and neighbors, and then to shut herself away in her home with her two sons. Together they were to pour out the only jar of oil that they had remaining in their possession. God miraculously multiplied the oil to fill all the vessels. The money gained from the sale of that oil was sufficient to pay the debt and to give the family the necessary money to live.

In one case, God immediately recovered a potential loss. In the other case, God required the woman and her sons to take specific steps which involved work and management of existing resources. I don't know how God will deal with you in resolving your indebtedness, but I believe this: He has a plan for helping you get out of debt. It may take a miracle, but God is a miracle worker. Seek His counsel. Both the prophet's son and the prophet's widow had the good sense to seek out godly counsel as they faced their financial difficulty. We are wise to do the same.

And the sons of the prophets said to Elisha, "See now, the place where we dwell with you is too small for us. Please, let us go to the Jordan, and let every man take a beam from there, and let us make there a place where we may dwell." So he answered, "Go." Then one said, "Please consent to go with your servants." And he answered, "I will go." So he went with them. And when they came to the Jordan, they cut down trees. But as one was cutting down a tree, the iron ax head fell into the water; and he cried out and said, "Alas, master! For it was borrowed." So the man of God said, "Where did it fall?" And he showed him the place. So he cut off a stick, and threw it in there; and he made the iron float. Therefore he said, "Pick it up for yourself." So he reached out his hand and took it.

—2 Kings 6:1–7

What work was the young man doing when the ax head got lost? Why did he become so upset? What does this reveal of his character?

What did the young man do when he found himself in trouble? What was his part in the recovery of the ax head? What principles do these things show concerning debt?

One of the ways in which God helps us to be free of debt is to give us an opportunity to increase our income. That opportunity may come in the form of a new job or a part-time job to augment the one that we currently have.

Some people jump quickly to the conclusion that the primary solution for their debt is to earn more money. That isn't always the case. The truth is, unless you change your habits and attitudes that got you into debt in the first place, an increase in income isn't likely to resolve your problem. You are likely to be in even greater debt, thinking that you now have the ability to pay your old bills and take on new ones. Again, ask the Lord to give you His wisdom in the matter of your income.

As You Face Your Debts

Be resolved to pay your debts. Don't seek to escape them. Don't ignore them. Set a goal date for the payment of each bill. Work steadily, consistently, and patiently toward full payment of what you owe.

Thank God for His help as you pay off each bill. Make the payment of your debts an opportunity for praise. Don't complain about the bills that remain or criticize yourself or others for your indebtedness. Review your financial expenditures weekly. Take a long look at how you became a victim of debt, and make the necessary changes in your credit card, borrowing, and spending habits.

Once you are free from debt, praise God for helping you to be free of financial bondage. Ask for God's continual help so that you might live debt-free for the rest of your life. Trust Him to guide you and to help you.

> Render therefore to all their due: taxes to whom taxes are due, customs to whom customs, fear to whom fear, honor to whom honor. Owe no one anything except to love one another, for he who loves another has fulfilled the law.
>
> —Romans 13:7–8

Note that Paul admonishes us to pay our bills, including taxes and other recurring debts. How is this different from financial bondage?

How can a person avoid financial bondage by following Paul's commandment in these verses?

⚘ Today and Tomorrow ⚘

TODAY: THE LORD DOES NOT WANT ME TO BE IN FINANCIAL BONDAGE.

TOMORROW: I WILL BEGIN THIS WEEK TO WORK DILIGENTLY AT BRINGING DOWN MY DEBT.

The Key to Unlocking Prosperity

Part 1

─── ❧ **In This Lesson** ☙ ───

LEARNING: WHAT DOES GOD EXPECT FROM ME?

GROWING: HOW DO I OPEN MYSELF UP TO GOD?

Laziness, debt, and bad spending habits are major reasons that people do not enjoy the prosperity that God desires for them. The number one reason, however, is that people withhold from God. They withhold their hearts and their wills, refusing to obey God's principles. They stubbornly make their own decisions, refusing to avail themselves of God's wisdom. They withhold what resources they do have, refusing to let loose of any of it because they don't trust God to provide for them. Stingy, self-centered people cannot prosper. It is like asking a turtle to walk to freedom while it is all closed up inside its shell. It can't be done.

Being open to God involves both giving to and receiving from God. We give Him our praise, our abilities, our resources, and we ask God to use us. God uses us when we make ourselves available to Him, and He blesses us by returning all that we need physically, mentally, and materially. The person who closes himself off from God may want things from God, but he does not want to give anything to God in return. Usually, that person wants only very specific things from God. This is not true receiving.

When we receive from God, we are open to receiving whatever He has for us with a thankful heart. There is no true receiving from God without the balance of giving to God. It's like having a wide-open door that allows passage in both directions.

God doesn't want merely your money. Many people see God as having a giant hand extended toward them, ready to take whatever they have. That picture cannot be supported with Scripture. It is the notion of selfish mankind. God wants all of you. He wants a life totally and completely committed to Him in love and service, a life dedicated to doing things God's way and to being God's person on this earth. God wants a relationship with you that holds nothing back. And in return, He desires to hold nothing of Himself back from you.

Who gets the better end of this covenant relationship? You do, of course. You are a finite, imperfect person. God receives you as you are. He gives you in return all of who He is—infinite, perfect. He asks you to receive Him in fullness. And when you do, you can't help prospering.

> A father of the fatherless, a defender of widows, is God in His holy habitation. God sets the solitary in families; He brings out those who are bound into prosperity; But the rebellious dwell in a dry land.
>
> —Psalm 68:5–6

How is it a sign of rebelliousness to close yourself off from God? To want His blessings without obeying His commands?

Three Reasons Why You Withhold from God

There are three main reasons why you withhold your life, including your resources, from God. All of them have deeply spiritual ramifications.

1. You want to do things your own way. You act out of human pride. You want what you want, and you want to keep everything that you have earned. Rebellion against God's plan and principles is always an expression of personal pride. The basis for pride is that you think you are somebody, and that you have acquired the substance of your life, apart from God. Nothing could be farther from the truth.

Everything that you have comes from God—all of your talents, your good ideas, your energy, your very life's breath. You may think that you exist and act and produce apart from God, but you don't. God cannot bless a proud heart. Such a heart is closed to God's work. The rebellious person is in no position to become prosperous.

A man's pride will bring him low, But the humble in spirit will retain honor.

—Proverbs 29:23

What does it mean to be "humble in spirit"? Give practical examples.

⮞ When have you seen someone's pride bring him low? When has your own pride brought you low?

2. You have unbelief. A second reason that you withhold your life and substance from God is that you don't trust God to provide for you or to take care of you. You refuse to believe that God's promises and principles apply to you personally. You think that you have to do it yourself because God either can't or won't.

Again, nothing could be farther from the truth. You will come quickly to the end of yourself—to the end of your ability, the end of your power, the end of your life. When you trust in yourself, you trust in someone who is frail, weak, and temporary—no matter how strong and great you may think yourself at the moment. When you trust in God, however, you put your trust in Someone who is all-powerful, all-knowing, and eternal. He doesn't fail. He doesn't change. In God is the greatest security that you can ever know. Anytime you are tempted to think that you cannot trust God to take care of you:

> Consider the ravens, for they neither sow nor reap, which have neither storehouse nor barn; and God feeds them. Of how much more value are you than the birds? And which of you by worrying can add one cubit to his stature? If you then are not able to do the least, why are you anxious for the rest? Consider the

lilies, how they grow: they neither toil nor spin; and yet I say to you, even Solomon in all his glory was not arrayed like one of these. If then God so clothes the grass, which today is in the field and tomorrow is thrown into the oven, how much more will He clothe you, O you of little faith? And do not seek what you should eat or what you should drink, nor have an anxious mind. For all these things the nations of the world seek after, and your Father knows that you need these things. But seek the kingdom of God, and all these things shall be added to you. Do not fear, little flock, for it is your Father's good pleasure to give you the kingdom.

—Luke 12:24–32

For the LORD God is a sun and shield; The LORD will give grace and glory; No good thing will He withhold from those who walk uprightly. O LORD of hosts, Blessed is the man who trusts in You!

—Psalm 84:11–12

What does it mean to walk uprightly? How can a person know whether his life is upright?

❧ Why does the Lord require us to walk uprightly before He will pour out "good things" into our lives?

3. You are unthankful. You may withhold yourself from God because you have an ungrateful heart. You know deep inside that God is sovereign and the Source of your life. You believe in God and trust Him to the best of your ability. But then you never give Him a word of thanks. You never open your mouth to praise Him or to acknowledge His work in your life.

When you fail to voice your thanksgiving and praise to God, you fail to give Him what is rightfully due. God alone is worthy of praise. In fact, Jesus noted that, if you don't praise the Lord, the very stones will cry out and do so. (See Luke 19:40.) God desires your praise, not because it satisfies any need in Him, but because it opens you up to receive from God. When you praise God, you have a much clearer understanding of who He is, and who you are, and a much greater appreciation of all that He has done for you. Praise keeps you cleansed of pride. It keeps you in a right relationship with God.

> You are worthy, O Lord, to receive glory and honor and power;
> For You created all things, and by Your will they exist and were created.
>
> —Revelation 4:11

❧ Why is God worthy of our praise and honor? Why should *you* praise Him?

🕭 Spend time right now praising and thanking the Lord for all that He has done for you—including giving you life another day.

The Lord simply does not prosper anyone who is rebellious, proud, unbelieving, or unthankful. Such a person has closed himself to God and is in no position to receive from God. Ask the Lord today to keep you from pride. Ask Him to help you trust Him more. Praise the Lord today for all that He has done for you and through you, and praise Him for His many promises of good things yet to come.

Withholding Our Substance from God

A part of withholding yourself from the Lord invariably includes withholding your substance from God. You miss out on prosperity when you do not give of your material goods to God—including your money. It is not enough that you give God your heart, time, and talents. Your material substance is also a part of you. In many ways, it is a *tangible* expression of *intangible* time, energy, and ability. You have what you hold in your hands because God has given you the ability to earn it; money is earned in exchange for time and skills. Money is a part of you, both in earning it and in giving it. You must be as generous in your material gifts as you are in every other area.

Giving opens up the financial area of your life to God. If you want to be blessed financially, you must be generous in your finances. The degree to which you open up yourself to God in giving is the degree to which you open up yourself to God for receiving. If you are closed to God in your finances, you are also closed to God in reaping financial blessing.

He who sows sparingly will also reap sparingly, and he who sows bountifully will also reap bountifully.

—2 Corinthians 9:6

❧ Seeds naturally grow plants—the more you sow, the more you grow. Why does Paul use this analogy to discuss giving money to the Lord?

❧ Do you tithe regularly? Do you give generously or grudgingly?

❧ Today and Tomorrow ❧

TODAY: THE LORD WANTS ME TO GIVE MYSELF TO HIM COMPLETELY AND FREELY.

TOMORROW: I WILL ASK THE LORD TO SHOW ME THIS WEEK ANY AREAS OF MY LIFE WHICH I HAVE CLOSED TO HIM.

The Key to Unlocking Prosperity

Part 2

℞ **In This Lesson** ℞

LEARNING: ISN'T MY MONEY MY OWN TO USE AS I SEE FIT?

GROWING: HOW MUCH AM I SUPPOSED TO TITHE?

God has set forth very specific directions about what He expects us to give of our finances. One of the clearest Bible passages is Malachi 3:8–12:

> "Will a man rob God?
> Yet you have robbed Me!
> But you say,
> 'In what way have we robbed You?'
> In tithes and offerings.
> You are cursed with a curse,
> For you have robbed Me,
> Even this whole nation.
> Bring all the tithes into the storehouse,
> That there may be food in My house,
> And try Me now in this,"
> Says the Lord of hosts,
> "If I will not open for you the windows of heaven

And pour out for you such blessing
That there will not be room enough to receive it.
And I will rebuke the devourer for your sakes,
So that he will not destroy the fruit of your ground,
Nor shall the vine fail to bear fruit for you in the field,"
Says the Lord of hosts;
"And all nations will call you blessed,
For you will be a delightful land,"
Says the Lord of hosts.

Let's take a close look at several key concepts presented in this passage.

✎ Tithes and Offerings ✎

This passage gives us God's direction on how to give to Him—the tithe, which is ten percent. (The word *tithe* is based on the number ten in Hebrew.) Offerings were gifts, often of material goods, that were given above and beyond the tithe. Offerings were usually made for specific reasons—to meet a special need in the nation or in thanksgiving for a special blessing. For example, the children of Israel gave an offering when the tabernacle was constructed. They gave so generously that Moses actually had to tell them to stop giving! (See Ex. 35:4-36:7.)

The tithe was expected to be the first tenth of what a person had received. If we were counting out pennies, we would say, "One for God, nine for me. One for God, nine for me." At no time in the Scriptures is the first tenth considered to belong rightfully to anyone other than God. The tithe is given to God *from* our increase and *for* our increase. It is the way that we open the door of our finances to give and then to receive God's blessing.

We should always keep in mind that God gives us this tenth in the first place. It never is ours. Remember the words of 1 Chronicles 29:14: "All things come from You, and of Your own we have given You." When we give the first tenth of our earnings back to God, we return to Him what was His in the first place, and what He asks us to give to Him so that He might give us even more. The tithe is our way to renew God's blessing into our lives. It is always for our increase. This cyclical aspect of giving is well stated in Isaiah 55:10–11:

> For as the rain comes down,
> and the snow from heaven,
> And do not return there,
> But water the earth,
> And make it bring forth and bud,
> That it may give seed to the sower
> And bread to the eater,
> So shall My word be that goes forth from My mouth;
> It shall not return to Me void,
> But it shall accomplish what I please,
> And it shall prosper in the thing for which I sent it.

God gives you His blessings, including material provision, and whatever He gives to you has the seed to produce even more blessing. The rain and snow cause the plants to grow and produce for your benefit, just as His Word has the potential to produce faith in your heart. His material blessing has the potential to bring you even greater blessing. If you hoard that seed of potential blessing and keep it for yourself, it will not produce. You cannot make that seed grow. Only God can cause a seed of any kind to multiply on your behalf.

> Honor the LORD with your possessions, And with the firstfruits of all your increase; So your barns will be filled with plenty, And your vats will overflow with new wine.

> —Proverbs 3:9–10

🕮 What does it mean to "honor the Lord with your posses-sions"? How is this done?

🕮 Most of us are not farmers, so how do we honor the Lord with our "firstfruits"? Give practical examples.

Giving tithes and offerings was to be marked by joy; the presenting of tithes and offerings was a celebration in response to what God had given and in anticipation of what God would give. The Lord is very specific in the way that we are to give our tithes and offerings.

First, we are to bring our tithes and offerings into His storehouse. That generally referred to His tabernacle in the Old Testament, and the church in the New Testament. Our tithes are to be given where we worship the Lord. It is to be a place with His name on it—not a mere charitable work, but a work that bears the Lord's name.

Second, we are to make our gifts on a regular basis. Paul advised the Corinthians, "On the first day of the week let each one of you lay something aside, storing up as he may prosper, that there be no collections when I come" (1 Cor. 16:2). The giving of the believers was to be a regular part of their weekly worship service.

Third, we are to make our gifts joyfully. People who give grudgingly, from a sense of obligation and duty, are not opening up their entire lives to God's prosperity. Hear the words of Paul to the Corinthians:

> So let each one give as he purposes in his heart, not grudgingly or of necessity; for God loves a cheerful giver. And God is able to make all grace abound toward you, that you, always having all sufficiency in all things, may have an abundance for every good work.
>
> —2 Corinthians 9:7–8

When have you given money to the Lord's work with a grudging spirit? With a cheerful spirit? How did the experiences differ?

According to these verses, what is God's purpose in blessing us with "all sufficiency in all things"? What does this suggest about His priorities for our money?

The joy in our hearts is a direct expression of our trust in God to meet our needs. "But," you may ask, "all of these references to tithing are in the Old Testament. I'm a New Testament believer, and I don't see much about tithing in the New Testament." There is a reason for that. Jesus certainly taught that we are to give:

~ to the needy (Matt. 25:37-40).

~ sacrificially (Mark 12:41-44).

~ without a great public display or show (Matt. 6:1-4).

~ expecting to receive in proportion to what we give (Luke 6:38).

~ knowing that it is more blessed to give than to receive (Acts 20:35).

Jesus didn't teach about tithing because the people were already tithing. Tithing was deeply ingrained in the society in which Jesus ministered. There was no reason to preach about something that the people were already doing. In fact, the deeply religious Pharisees were tithing the herbs that grew in their gardens. Jesus didn't decry their tithing in that manner; instead, He approved of their tithing but said that they were to place greater importance on bigger issues: God's justice and the love of God. He said, "You tithe mint and rue and all manner of herbs, and pass by justice and the love of God. These you ought to have done, without leaving the others undone" (Luke 11:42).

The first-century Christians were giving Christians. They tithed to the storehouse of the Lord, and in some cases they sacrificed all that they had for the benefit of their brothers and sisters in Christ. (See Acts 4:34–37.) The early Christians did not balk at the requirement to give. They rejoiced in the opportunity.

Romans 12:8 speaks of a divine gift of giving. Paul tells those who have this ministry of giving to give "with liberality." Those who are called to such a ministry go beyond giving tithes and offerings. They are often blessed in unusual and abundant ways so that they can give great sums to the work of the Lord. Sometimes they are blessed for a season in their lives so that they can give special gifts to particular ministries. I know of a man who was giving God 90 percent of what he earned and living off the remaining 10 percent. His income had grown so vast over the years of faithful giving that he was able to live a very fine life on the 10 percent. He channeled everything else into the work of the Lord. This man had a gift of giving.

> And with great power the apostles gave witness to the resur-
> rection of the Lord Jesus. And great grace was upon them all.
> Nor was there anyone among them who lacked; for all who
> were possessors of lands or houses sold them, and brought
> the proceeds of the things that were sold, and laid them at
> the apostles' feet; and they distributed to each as anyone had
> need.

> —Acts 4:33–35

☙ When have you known of someone who gave to the Lord at great cost to himself?

☙ What motivated these early Christians to give so generously to the Lord's work?

97

❧ Robbing God ☙

Few of us would ever think of robbing God. We tend to think that we will benefit ourselves if we withhold money from God, and we rarely see our failure to give as robbing God. Yet God says that, when we withhold our tithes and offerings, we are robbing Him. The tithe belongs to God. It is holy. (See Lev. 27:30.) It is sanctified and rightfully belongs to God. When we take God's portion of our earnings and use it for ourselves, we are taking what does not belong to us. God cannot bless thieves.

It is foolish to steal from God. God knows what you have, He knows where to find you and your resources, and He knows when you attempt to hide what is His. In attempting to cheat God, you are cheating yourself. You are cutting yourself off from His abundance.

❧ Food in God's House ☙

In Malachi, we read that we are to bring our tithes into God's storehouse so that there might be food in God's house. Can you imagine what would happen in our churches and in our nation if every Christian tithed on a regular basis? There would be an enormous amount of money for spreading the gospel and helping needy people. Outreach programs to poor, sick, and destitute people would be fully funded. Christian charities would have the money that they need and would not have to spend their time or resources on fund-raising. Missionaries and evangelistic missions would be fully supported. The increased proclamation of the gospel would have a tremendous impact on strengthening the moral fiber of our nation, and especially on strengthening our families. The net result would be far less need and far less crime in our society, which could translate into lower taxes, less dependence on programs such as Social Security and Medicare, and less expensive bureaucracy.

The tithe doesn't evaporate into thin air. It is used to benefit people in need and to support those who minister directly to them. It is used for programs that give life and hope to those in need. The tithe comes back to us indirectly by giving us healthier and more vibrant communities (both churches and neighborhoods). Malachi said that the nation of Israel was under a curse because it had robbed God of tithes and offerings. We are no different today.

> "Bring all the tithes into the storehouse, that there may be food in My house, and try Me now in this," says the LORD of hosts, "If I will not open for you the windows of heaven and pour out for you such blessing that there will not be room enough to receive it."
>
> —Malachi 3:10

❧ God is Lord over all creation, and He does not need anything that man can offer. Why, then, does He call His people to bring tithes?

❧ Have you been robbing God of what is due to Him? How will you change that in the coming week?

99

☙ A Test of God's Faithfulness ❧

God almost dares us in this passage of Malachi to put His faithfulness to the test. He says, "Try Me now in this." In other words, "Put Me to the test. Check it out for yourself." God has given us a system that is so easy that even a child can do it. Are you willing to give God ten percent on a regular basis and see what happens?

☙ A Blessing from Heaven ❧

God promises that He will open the windows of heaven and "pour out for you such blessing that there will not be room enough to receive it" if you will bring your tithes to His storehouse. That blessing is different for each person, but it certainly comes to us in the form of:

☙ an abundance of strength, energy, and physical health.

☙ an abundance of creative ideas and insights.

☙ a renewed joy and positive attitude.

☙ an enhanced ability to communicate with others and work with them.

☙ provision from unexpected sources.

☙ new opportunities for work and investment.

Furthermore, God says that the blessing is so great that you will not be able to contain it. Have you ever enjoyed a blessing that great? And again, note what happens: this increase overflows from your life to bless others. When you prosper, everybody around you is brought to a higher level of prosperity, including those who have a lack in their lives.

❧ A Rebuke to the Devourer ❧

God promises an overflowing blessing, and He says that He will "rebuke the devourer." Your work will come to fruition. You will be spared from attacks of the enemy against your life. In very practical ways, a rebuke to the devourer can mean:

❧ less illness, less susceptibility to viruses and disease-causing bacteria.

❧ fewer breakdowns in equipment, machinery, or vehicles.

❧ fewer obstacles or problems encountered.

❧ fewer interruptions, delays, or detours.

❧ fewer accidents or mishaps.

All of that can result in fewer lost days at work, less stress, and lower expenses. You will experience a beneficial increase when you give your tithes and offerings, and you will experience a decrease in things that cause you loss or harm. The net effect is altogether positive! There is another way to look at this: the 90 percent that is remaining after you give God His 10 percent will have the blessing of God. It will be a full 90 percent that has the potential to bring great reward. Believe me, I would rather have 90 percent with God's blessing than 100 percent without God's blessing.

> But when you do a charitable deed, do not let your left hand know what your right hand is doing, that your charitable deed may be in secret; and your Father who sees in secret will Himself reward you openly.
>
> —Matthew 6:3–4

101

What does it mean to keep your left hand from knowing what your right is doing? How is this done when tithing? When serving others?

Why is it important to perform charitable deeds in secret?

Honor

When you bring all your tithes and offerings into God's storehouse, you experience the reward of a good reputation. The Lord says, "And all nations will call you blessed." In other words, your life will be enviable. Others will speak well of you and want to be like you.

This directly relates to your Christian witness. When people see you prospering, they will gravitate toward you. They will want to know your secret. They will want to have the joy that you have, the fulfillment and meaning that you enjoy, the blessings that you are experiencing. You will find it easier than ever in your life to share the gospel of Jesus Christ with others.

❧ Four Promises ☙

Giving tithes and offerings holds out these four promises in Malachi:

1. Prosperity: the windows of heaven will be opened to you.

2. Plenty: your blessing will be overflowing.

3. Protection: the devourer will be rebuked for your sake.

4. Personal Testimony: you will have an expanded witness for the Lord.

You should be eager to give to God what is rightfully His, given these promises! You should be excited and enthusiastic about giving—not merely so that you might receive financial blessing but so that you can receive God's presence.

With God's blessing, you always receive God's presence. Your relationship with Him grows richer, deeper, more meaningful, and more intimate. God's blessings are bestowed upon you so that God might prove Himself faithful and so that He might draw you ever nearer to Himself. That is the greatest reward that you can ever know.

A Life That Is Above and Beyond

I have never tithed. In my first job, I made $4 a week as a newspaper boy. I brought $1 a week to God's storehouse. I never would have dreamed of limiting myself to a mere 40 cents. I was so grateful for the job and so pleased to be earning $4 that it never crossed my mind to give less than $1. Shortly thereafter, I got a job—also as a newspaper boy—for $20 a week. Talk about the windows of heaven opening to me! That was a fivefold increase in my income! I gave back far more than 10 percent a week to the church.

While I had that job, a man offered to help me attend college. I went to college with $75 in my pocket, and I left college not owing a cent. God richly and abundantly met my need. Once I had only a dime in my pocket, but I was never completely without money. And I never gave *only* 10 percent of what I received to God. I was in relationship with a God of abundance. I never would have dreamed of giving back to Him only a bare minimum.

My giving was born of gratitude and thanksgiving that He should do so much for me. My only regrets were that I couldn't give more to the work of the Lord. I know from personal experience that God is a God of blessing. He doesn't want your money as some kind of payback for blessing you. He wants you. He wants you to want Him. He wants you to open up your life so that your entire existence is one of generous giving and abundant receiving. He wants you to grow and prosper in every area of your life. Our God is a loving God who desires your utmost and highest. Are you willing to trust Him today with your money and material resources? The key to unlocking prosperity lies in what you give.

> And remember the words of the Lord Jesus, that He said, "It is more blessed to give than to receive."
>
> —Acts 20:35

When have you experienced this principle in your own life?

What are some of the blessings that we receive when we give?

Today and Tomorrow

TODAY: THE LORD WANTS ME TO GIVE HIM WHAT IS HIS BY RIGHT, IN-CLUDING MY TITHES.

TOMORROW: I WILL TAKE THE LORD'S CHALLENGE TO HEART THIS WEEK, AND WILL GIVE TO HIM GENEROUSLY.

LESSON 9

Danger Signals

―― ❧ In This Lesson ❧ ――

LEARNING: WHAT HAPPENED TO THE PROSPERITY I HAD?

GROWING: HOW CAN I PROSPER AND KEEP ON PROSPERING?

You can lose the blessings that God gives you. Prosperity is not necessarily a constant state of being. It is not enough to know how to become prosperous in God's eyes, you must also learn how to stay prosperous. It is only as you live in prosperity that you can become an outstanding steward of all that God gives you. Keeping prosperity is certainly at the heart of good financial stewardship.

God gives only good gifts, and all God's gifts are good. But it is equally true that we can misuse all of God's good gifts. Food is a necessity, but too much food can make us fat, which in turn can contribute to disease. Medicines are good, but they can cause harm when taken wrong. Affection is wonderful, but it can destroy a family when directed inappropriately. We must be very cautious to use the blessings that God has given us for good and not evil.

❧ When have you seen someone misuse a blessing of God? What was the result?

Five Attitudes That Eat Away at Prosperity

Five attitudes can destroy prosperity, usually bit by bit until all of a blessing has been eaten away.

1. Covetousness

Covetousness can also be defined as greed. In an earlier lesson, we discussed how greed can keep us from being prosperous. It is also possible for covetousness to develop once we enjoy prosperity. Jesus told a parable that illustrated this:

> Then one from the crowd said to Him, "Teacher, tell my brother to divide the inheritance with me." But He said to him, "Man, who made Me a judge or an arbitrator over you?" And He said to them, "Take heed and beware of covetousness, for one's life does not consist in the abundance of the things he possesses." Then He spoke a parable to them, saying: "The ground of a certain rich man yielded plentifully. And he thought within himself, saying, 'What shall I do, since I have no room to store my crops?' So he said, 'I will do this: I will pull down my barns and build greater, and there I will store all my crops and my goods. And I will say to my soul, "Soul, you have many goods laid up for many years; take your ease; eat, drink, and be merry." ' But God said to him, 'Fool! This night your soul will be required of you; then whose will those things be which you have provided?' So is he who lays up treasure for himself, and is not rich toward God."
>
> —Luke 12:13–21

Note the context for this parable. A man asked Jesus to tell his brother to divide an inheritance with him. The man who came to Jesus was very likely a younger brother, and the inheritance was likely the inheritance that went to the eldest brother—which was a double share. The younger brother no doubt wanted more than he was owed under the law of Moses; in other words, he was asking for something that was not rightfully his. He wanted the reward of more inheritance without the responsibility that went with it. (The double inheritance to a firstborn son also carried with it many family responsibilities.)

Jesus could tell that the man's request was rooted in covetousness. The same is true for any person who wants something for nothing. Such a person is greedy. He covets what is not rightfully his—what he has not earned, what he does not deserve, what he has not been given.

The greedy, covetous person begins to think that his possessions are his security, even his very identity. His wealth says to the world and to himself, "Look who I am." Your identity is always to be in Christ Jesus, not in things, status, or other relationships. A covetous spirit moves you away from intimacy with God and into a state of pride, which is the second attitude that you must avoid.

☙ Why did Jesus ask the young man who had made Him a judge over the brothers? What was at the root of the young man's request?

☙ What does it mean to be "rich toward God"? How is this wealth attained?

2. Pride

Jesus taught a parable to the covetous brother which spoke directly to the dangers of pride. Reread the passage from Luke. Circle the words *I* and *my* as you read the verses.

The proud person believes that he has earned all that he has; therefore, he has sole right to what he has. Jesus taught first that the rich man in this parable had great wealth because his land "yielded plentifully." It was a good year for farming; however, he saw the crops as *his* crops, the barns as *his* barns, all of the income as *his* income. There was no mention of giving God the firstfruits of the harvest, or any portion of it. He was totally self-contained and self-absorbed. He spoke totally to himself, about himself.

When you begin to take pride in your prosperity, you take credit for an achievement that is not totally your own. You rob God of the tithe and offerings owed to Him, and you presume to rob God of the glory owed His name. God will not prosper anyone who presumes to take the praise that is rightfully God's alone.

3. Selfishness

The rich man in the parable became selfish. He hoarded what he had. His possessions began to possess him. Selfish people rarely are generous toward God. I have met very few selfish people who tithe regularly; if they tithe, they do so grudgingly and without joy, and they reap virtually no spiritual blessing from their giving.

We all know what happens to a lake that has no outlet. It becomes slimy, and eventually all life within it is killed. The selfish person gradually dies on the inside, and his prosperity grows stale and withers away.

4. Presumption

Prosperous people must also guard against becoming presumptuous, an attitude that says, "I am owed this prosperity." They think that they have earned prosperity or that they are deserving of prosperity because of something that they have done.

God delights in giving to you, but at no time is He indebted to you. You must remain humble at all times, recognizing that all your life, including every breath you take and every beat of your heart, is according to God's grace and will. God is never required to serve you; at all times you are His servant. Presumption is a close cousin to pride.

> Better is the poor who walks in his integrity than one perverse
> in his ways, though he be rich.

—Proverbs 28:6

❧ What does it mean to walk in one's integrity? How is this different from being "perverse in his ways"?

❧ Why is it better to be poor and faithful than rich and perverse? What does this teach about God's definition of prosperity?

5. Pleasure

The rich man in Jesus' parable said, "Soul, you have many goods laid up for many years; take your ease; eat, drink, and be merry." The man decided to take his prosperity and live off it for the rest of his life. He had no desire to put forth any more effort. There is no mention of any desire to work for God. He wanted an easy life, and he presumed that he had many years to live.

God responded, "Fool! This night your soul will be required of you; then whose will those things be which you have provided?" No one can count on tomorrow. Our time on earth is in God's hands. We are to work with all our energy and ability every day of our lives. If we are not working in a career that produces income for ourselves, we certainly should be active in a volunteer ministry that benefits others. There is no retirement from being a productive member of the kingdom of God or from being an active witness to God's love. The rich man in Jesus' parable lost out materially and spiritually. God called him a fool.

> Where do wars and fights come from among you? Do they not come from your desires for pleasure that war in your members? You lust and do not have. You murder and covet and cannot obtain. You fight and war. Yet you do not have because you do not ask. You ask and do not receive, because you ask amiss, that you may spend it on your pleasures.
>
> —James 4:1–3

᠅ Why does James say that desires for pleasures "war in your members"? What does that mean? How does it happen?

🔖 What are the requirements for answered prayer, according to these verses? What attitudes prevent us from receiving what we pray for?

Ask the Lord to help you stay free of the following:

🔖 A covetous spirit

🔖 Pride

🔖 Selfishness or self-centeredness

🔖 Presumption that God owes you prosperity

🔖 A desire to live only for your ease, comfort, or pleasure

People who have these attitudes are in danger of having their possessions possess them, their goals become their gods, and their desires destroy them.

Five Warning Signs that You Must Heed

You are in danger of losing your prosperity if any one of these conditions begins to characterize your life:

1. You consider money to be the consistency of your life rather than the sustenance. You do not use money merely to sustain your life; your life consists of abundant possessions that you constantly think about. I once heard about a man who no longer had room to contain all of God's blessings. He found that he was occupied all the time with concerns about the maintenance of his three homes and five automobiles, not to mention his fishing and ski boats, his two snowmobiles, and his small airplane. Something always seemed to need maintenance or remodeling. He said, "There wasn't much time left for anything else except to be concerned about taxes and which expenses could be deducted. I decided to eliminate at least half of what I had owned in order to have time to enjoy the other half!" The consistency of the man's life had become wrapped up in things. He was wise to get rid of what he did.

You must never allow your possessions to grow beyond the sustenance level. You are in danger when all of your plans and ambitions are related to material goods.

> A faithful man will abound with blessings, but he who hastens
> to be rich will not go unpunished.
>
> —Proverbs 28:20

Why does the Lord punish those who "hasten to be rich"? Why is this sinful behavior?

In what ways is the faithful man different from someone who hastens to become rich? What motivates the faithful man? The man hastening toward wealth?

2. You begin to fall in love with money. Nobody sets out to love money. People usually drift into that position slowly and imperceptibly. Be aware of your growing desires for certain objects or a growing obsession to meet certain financial goals, including sales quotas and profit margins.

Falling in love with money includes falling in love with the idea of making money and with the things that money can buy. You daydream constantly about the things that you would like to own, and your mind is preoccupied with get-rich schemes and your plans to increase your income. The love of money leads to compromise of values. It leads to cutting corners in other important areas of your life so that you can devote more time and energy to your job or leisure time.

When you begin to love money, you are in danger. The Bible teaches, "The love of money is a root of all kinds of evil, for which some have strayed from the faith in their greediness, and pierced themselves through with many sorrows" (1 Tim. 6:10). We know that a love of money can result in the evil of crime. However, many evils that come from a love of money are much more subtle than that. Some of the sorrows may be feelings of:

- inner emptiness.

- disillusionment.

- disappointment.

- dissatisfaction.

- nagging frustrations and worries.

The sorrows may include destroyed relationships with business colleagues and family members. The sorrows may include a loss of intimacy with God.

3. You set out to be rich. Gaining wealth becomes your number one goal. You are in danger when the acquisition of money and material goods becomes the foremost ambition of your life. First Timothy 6:9 warns, "Those who desire to be rich fall into temptation and a snare, and into many foolish and harmful lusts which drown men in destruction and perdition."

If you want more than anything else to be wealthy, you become a prime target for every money-making scheme that comes along. Your judgment will be clouded regarding business associates. Your common sense will evaporate. You will be prone to temptation.

> For we brought nothing into this world, and it is certain we can carry nothing out. And having food and clothing, with these we shall be content. But those who desire to be rich fall into temptation and a snare, and into many foolish and harmful lusts which drown men in destruction and perdition.
>
> —1 Timothy 6:7–9

➤ What does it mean to drown in destruction? In perdition? How does a desire for wealth bring these things upon a person?

➤ Why does Paul mention that we "brought nothing into this world" in this context? Why does he mention that "we can carry nothing out"?

4. You become reckless in handling a blessing of money. When an unexpected financial blessing occurs, some people hoard that money, while others spend it with abandon. Both positions are dangerous. The Lord wants you to be generous, and He also wants you to be prudent. Give tithes and offerings to God's storehouse. Set aside a reasonable amount in savings. Invest wisely and spend wisely.

5. You look to your financial concerns more than to God's Word when making decisions. Let me share some very practical ways in which this may manifest itself:

> ✒ You visualize what money can do for you more than what God can do for you.

> ✒ You plan your life around your income instead of what God calls you to do.

> ✒ You feel that you have no time to hear God's Word or to participate in church activities.

> ✒ You look for get-rich schemes and rationalize why they might be good for you.

> ✒ You work for retirement ease rather than retirement service.

> ✒ You begin to designate certain possessions as solely for your personal use.

> ✒ You become discontented with your possessions, and desire things that you don't own.

↝ You spend more of your off-work time with people who are involved in your business than with your family and church friends.

↝ Your desire moves away from spending time with God to spending time dealing with money, investments, or new business ventures.

Pay attention to these warning signs. Refuse to yield to them. If you find that you are starting to develop these patterns in your life, ask God to forgive you and to help you return to the principles and habits that brought you to a prosperous position in the first place. Trust Him anew with your whole life, and ask Him to restore wholeness and prosperity that is first and foremost spiritual prosperity.

↝ Today and Tomorrow ↜

TODAY: THE LORD WILL REMOVE MY PROSPERITY IF IT INTERFERES WITH MY SPIRITUAL WELL-BEING.

TOMORROW: I WILL EXAMINE MY LIFE THIS WEEK, LOOKING FOR DANGER SIGNS IN MY ATTITUDE TOWARD MONEY.

The Wheel of Prosperity

God wants you to live a positive life in a negative world. He wants you to prosper. Many people don't experience prosperity because of tradition. People tend to be creatures of habits, some of which are long-standing. Tradition can be either a trap or a blessing. Jesus wasn't accepted as Messiah because the religious leaders of His day were locked into traditional beliefs that did not allow for a suffering, self-sacrificing Messiah. They were seeking a triumphant political leader, and their beliefs blinded them to the truth of Jesus as their Redeemer.

Part of the reason that more people don't experience prosperity is that people tend to gravitate toward what is safe, not necessarily what is good. Those who experience good often settle for good rather than pursuing what is better or best.

To be prosperous, you have to *want* to be prosperous. You have to want to live your life in obedience to God's plan and principles, and you have to want more for every area of your life, especially more for your spiritual life and your witness for Christ. When you ask God to lead you into the way of total prosperity, you have taken a major step toward prosperity. God answers and more than satisfies the heart that is hungry for Him and for His will.

> Blessed is the man who walks not in the counsel of the ungodly, Nor stands in the path of sinners, Nor sits in the seat of the scornful; But his delight is in the law of the LORD, And in His law he meditates day and night.

> —Psalm 1:1–2

☙ Notice the verbs in the first verse. What would it indicate if a person were walking, then stopped and stood, then sat with the ungodly?

☙ How does this progression apply to gradually establishing bad habits?

Making a Prosperity Wheel

I encourage you to make a wheel of prosperity. Draw a large circle on a large piece of paper. At the center of the circle, draw a smaller circle. Label the smaller circle "God." Then draw crosshairs over the circles so that you have divided both into four even quadrants. Label these four sections: "Family Life," "Social/Recreational Life," "Business Life," and "Spiritual Life."

Next, identify goals for each area of your life. If you don't set your goals, someone else will set them for you. Don't write your goals using words. Instead, use pictures. Find pictures in magazines that illustrate what you want. For example, if you want to study the Bible more, find a picture of a Bible or a picture of someone reading the Bible. If you want to spend more time with your family, find a picture of family members doing something together. If you can't find a picture that fits your goal, draw one.

After you have completed your wheel, put it in a place where you can refer to it often, such as the inside of a closet door. If you want your wheel to remain private, put it in a place "for your eyes only," perhaps a locked desk drawer.

Encourage other members of your family to make wheels of prosperity for their lives. (Your children might label the "Business Life" quadrant as "School Life.") And then come together as a family to make a wheel of prosperity that pertains to your family life as a whole. You may find that many of your goals are shared by other family members. Pray together as a family about which goals are most important to you.

Benefits from the Wheel

A wheel of prosperity will remind you to keep God at the center of your desires. The wheel will remind you that God is the Source of your prosperity. Seeing the word *God* in the midst of your goals will remind you that all of your resources, talent, and time comes from God. It will also remind you to ask God often to direct your goal setting, and to help you achieve the goals that are God-ordained.

A wheel of prosperity will compel you to adjust priorities in your life. If you see that you have many goals in one area of your life, but very few in another, you must face the fact that your life is lopsided. A wheel that is out of balance results in a bumpy ride! Furthermore, a wheel that is out of balance creates a wobble that will eventually cause the wheel to break apart.

Take a good look at what you desire. Make all of these goals a matter of prayer priority. As the Lord leads you, change your priorities and readjust your goals, perhaps coming up with new goals, until you feel that your wheel is balanced and approved by God.

As you look at your wheel of prosperity, begin by looking at the word *God* and spend a few moments dwelling on the goodness of God and His many benefits to you. Give Him thanks and praise. Ask Him to direct your attention to areas of your life that need adjustment. As your eyes scan your wheel, you are likely to feel drawn to a particular goal. Ask the Lord to give you His wisdom about this area of your life.

A wheel of prosperity allows you to take a look at your total life at a glance. When I made my first wheel of prosperity, I realized that I had very few social and recreational goals. That realization helped me face the fact that I was headed for stress overload and burnout. If someone had asked me, "Do you lead a balanced life?" I would have answered, "Sure I do." But seeing my wheel of prosperity out of balance made me reevaluate my use of time and resources, as well as my hopes, desires, and goals.

After you have made your wheel of prosperity, answer these questions:

➠ How do I feel about the balance of my wheel?

∽ Which area of my life have I emphasized in the past? Neglected? With what results?

∽ In what ways am I being challenged by God today?

Managing the Wheel

A wheel of prosperity helps in five ways:

1. *Visualization*. The wheel is based on the goodness of God and the goodness of His blessings to His people. Remind yourself always that "the earth is full of the goodness of the Lord" (Ps. 33:5). Ask the Lord to rule your imagination and to provide a glimpse of His plan for you and the blessings that He desires to give to you.

2. *Expectation*. The wheel is based on the promises of God. The Bible declares that "you do not have because you do not ask" (James 4:2). As you visualize and identify your goals, you are in a better position to ask God specifically for what you truly desire and then to look for His answer or provision.

3. *Motivation*. The wheel is based on the plan of God. Psalm 32:8 states:

> I will instruct you and teach you in the way you should go;
> I will guide you with My eye.

Make it your motivation to see your life as God sees it, and then to do what God guides you to do. Make Psalm 25:4-5 your prayer:

> Show me Your ways, O Lord;
> Teach me Your paths.

Lead me in Your truth and teach me,
For You are the God of my salvation;
On You I wait all the day.

❧ Look at your wheel of prosperity. How many of your goals involve God's guidance? How many involve your own efforts?

❧ Take time right now to ask the Lord for guidance and wisdom concerning your goals.

4. Meditation. The wheel is based on submission to God. As you meditate on God's Word, you learn more about the goodness of God and the goodness of His plan for your life. You must line up your personal plans and desires against the absolutes of God's Word. As 1 Thessalonians 5:21-22 admonishes, you must "test all things; hold fast what is good. Abstain from every form of evil." If at any time you find a Scripture that identifies one of your goals as being wrong before the Lord, you must remove it from your wheel.

5. Realization. The wheel is based on the faithfulness of God to guide you into all truth. He will impart His wisdom, and He will act for your eternal good. Remind yourself of God's promise: "All things work together for good to those who love God, to those who are the called according to His purpose" (Rom. 8:28).

A wheel of prosperity can help you open yourself to God and develop a greater dependency on Him. That's one of the reasons to construct it as a circle. Let it remind you always of God's desire that you be whole. Prosperity is rooted always in wholeness, growth, and fruitfulness.

It is not enough to believe in prosperity or visualize prosperity. Eventually, you must do the things that the Lord calls you to do. You must actually live out His plan. I encourage you to take that step today!

> And we know that all things work together for good to those who love God, to those who are the called according to His purpose.
>
> —Romans 8:28

What things in your life does God use to bring about good? What things is He using today, even if you can't see His final purpose?

Take time right now to ask the Lord to show you what He wants you to do this week to bring about His purposes for good in your life.

Today and Tomorrow

TODAY: THE LORD WANTS ME TO PROSPER FIRST AND FOREMOST IN MY RELATIONSHIP WITH HIM.

TOMORROW: I WILL MAKE A WHEEL OF PROSPERITY AND REFER TO IT FREQUENTLY IN THE COMING WEEKS.